WAR FOR THE PLAINS

✠

TIME® LIFE BOOKS

This volume is one of a series that chronicles the history and culture of the Native Americans. Other books in the series include:

THE FIRST AMERICANS
THE SPIRIT WORLD
THE EUROPEAN CHALLENGE
PEOPLE OF THE DESERT
THE WAY OF THE WARRIOR
THE BUFFALO HUNTERS
REALM OF THE IROQUOIS
THE MIGHTY CHIEFTAINS
KEEPERS OF THE TOTEM
CYCLES OF LIFE

The Cover: A Cheyenne horseman in a feathered headdress and two fellow tribesmen maintain a vigilant stance on their reservation in Montana in a photograph taken by Edward Curtis. The Cheyenne were among many Indian groups who were forced to cede their traditional lands and move onto reservations in the wake of the Plains war.

THE AMERICAN INDIANS

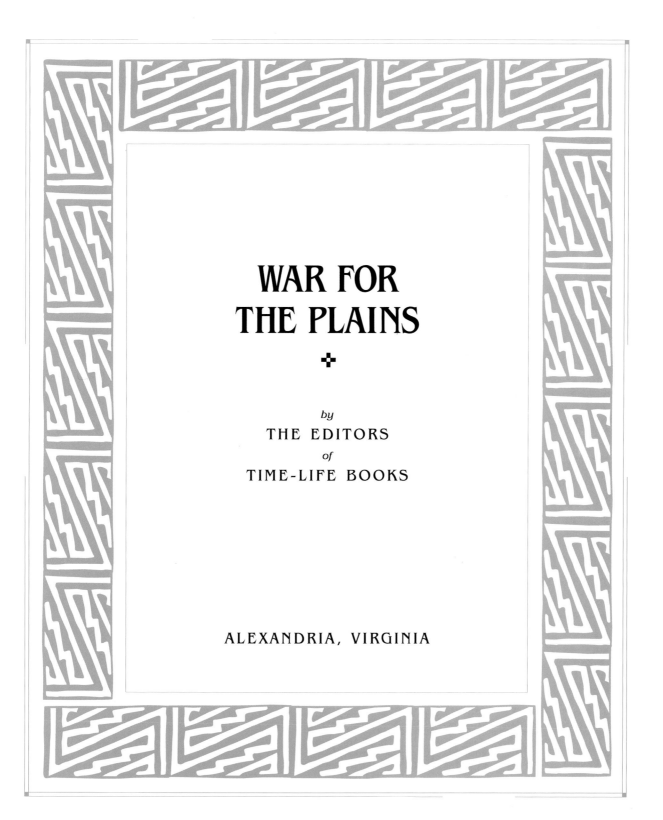

WAR FOR THE PLAINS

by
THE EDITORS
of
TIME-LIFE BOOKS

ALEXANDRIA, VIRGINIA

Library of Congress Cataloging in Publication Data
War for the plains/by the editors of Time-Life
Books.
  p.   cm.—(The American Indians)
  Includes bibliographical references (p.) and in-
dex.
  ISBN 0-8094-9445-0 (trade): $16.99.
  ISBN 0-8094-9446-9 (lib. bdg.)
  1. Indians of North America—Wars—1866-1895.
2. Indians of North America—Great Plains—Wars.
3. Indians of North America—Wars—1815-1875.
  I. Time-Life Books. II. Series.
E83.866.W24 1994   93-23449
973-dc20   CIP

THE AMERICAN INDIANS

SERIES EDITOR: Henry Woodhead
Administrative Editor: Jane Edwin

Editorial Staff for *War for the Plains*
Senior Art Directors: Dale Pollekoff (principal), Ray
Ripper
Picture Editor: Jane Coughran
Text Editor: Stephen G. Hyslop
Writer: Stephanie Lewis
Associate Editors/Research: Harris J. Andrews, Mary
Helena McCarthy (principals)
Assistant Editor/Research: Annette Scarpitta
Assistant Art Director: Susan M. Gibas
Senior Copyeditor: Ann Lee Bruen
Picture Coordinator: David Beard
Editorial Assistant: Gemma Villanueva

Special Contributors: Ronald H. Bailey, George G.
Daniels, Marfé Ferguson Delano, Tom Lewis, Brian
Pohanka, Lydia Preston, David S. Thomson, Gerald
P. Tyson (text); Martha Lee Beckington, Christine
Soares, Jennifer Veech (research); Barbara L. Klein
(index).

Correspondents: Elisabeth Kraemer-Singh (Bonn),
Christine Hinze (London), Christina Lieberman
(New York), Maria Vincenza Aloisi (Paris), Ann
Natanson (Rome). Valuable assistance was also
provided by: Elizabeth Brown, Daniel Donnelly
(New York).

General Consultants
Colonel John R. Elting, USA (Ret.), former associate
professor at West Point, was chief consultant to
the Time-Life Books CIVIL WAR series. His first association with Native Americans was during his
early years while living in Montana, first near the
Blackfeet, Flathead, and Shoshone reservations
and later near the Crow Agency. Colonel Elting has
written or edited more than 20 books, including
Amateurs, To Arms: A History of the War of 1812 and
Napoleonic Military Uniforms.

Frederick E. Hoxie is director of the D'Arcy Mc-
Nickle Center for the History of the American Indian at the Newberry Library in Chicago. Dr. Hoxie is
the author of *A Final Promise: The Campaign to As-
similate the Indians 1880-1920* and other works. He
has served as a history consultant to the
Cheyenne River and Standing Rock Sioux tribes,
Little Big Horn College archives, and the Senate
Select Committee on Indian Affairs. He is a trustee
of the National Museum of the American Indian in
Washington, D.C.

Darrell Robes Kipp, a Blackfeet Indian and great-
grandson of Chief Heavy Runner, is a founder and
director of the Piegan Institute in Browning, Montana, a private, nonprofit, tribally chartered organization that researches, promotes, and preserves
Native American languages, specifically the Blackfeet language. A graduate of Eastern Montana College and Harvard University, Mr. Kipp has for many
years served his tribe as a teacher, administrator,
technical writer, and historian. He has also worked
for the Maliseet Indian tribe of New Brunswick,
Canada, the Navajo, and the Confederated Assiniboin and Gros Ventre tribes, among others. Mr.

Kipp has written articles and produced materials
for video on the Blackfeet tribe.

Robert M. Utley is a historian who was with the
National Park Service for 25 years. During that
time, he served in various capacities, including
historian of the Southwest Region and chief historian in Washington, D.C. From 1977 until his retire-
ment in 1980, he was deputy executive director of
the President's Advisory Council on Historic
Preservation. Since then Mr. Utley has devoted
much of his time to historical research and writing
on the American West, focusing on military and
Indian aspects. Among his many books are *The
Lance and the Shield: The Life and Times of Sitting
Bull; Cavalier in Buckskin: George Armstrong Custer
and the Western Military Frontier;* and *The Indian
Frontier of the American West.* In 1988 Mr. Utley
was awarded the Western History Association
Prize for his published writings.

Special Consultants
Brian Pohanka is a historian and writer specializ-
ing in the American Civil War and the military history of the American West. He is the author of several books and numerous articles, including
studies of the U.S. Army-Indian conflict of 1876.
Mr. Pohanka also contributed to a biography of
Captain Miles Keogh, an Irish officer killed at Little
Bighorn. He is a life member of the Custer Battlefield Historical and Museum Association and has
participated in two archaeological investigations
of the Little Bighorn battlefield.

Arthur Silberman, director of the Native American
Painting Reference Library in Oklahoma City, has
written extensively Native American art and has
curated several museum exhibitions, including
"Beyond the Prison Gates: The Fort Marion Experience and Its Artistic Legacy." Mr. Silberman is also
a faculty member of Oklahoma City University
where he teaches a course in Native American
art history.

CONTENTS

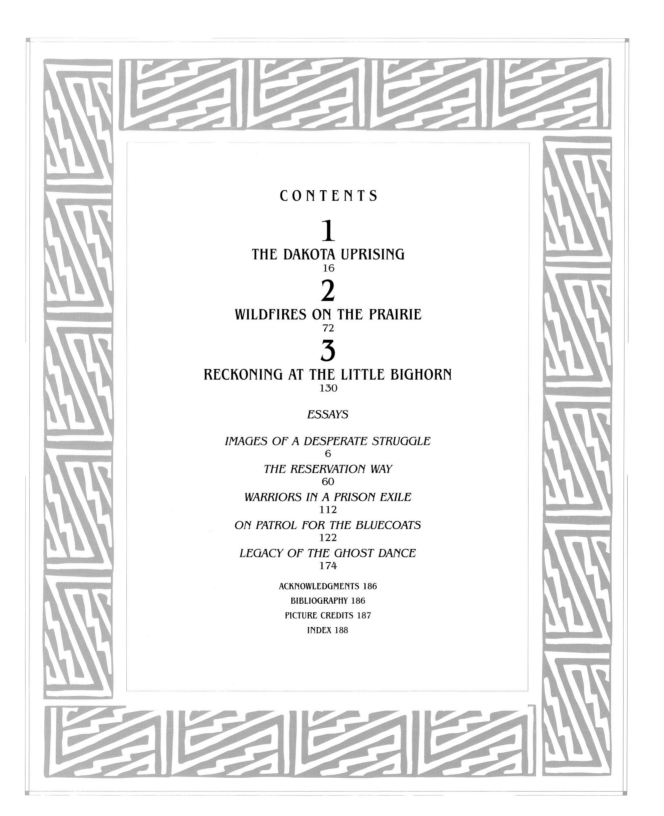

IMAGES OF A DESPERATE STRUGGLE

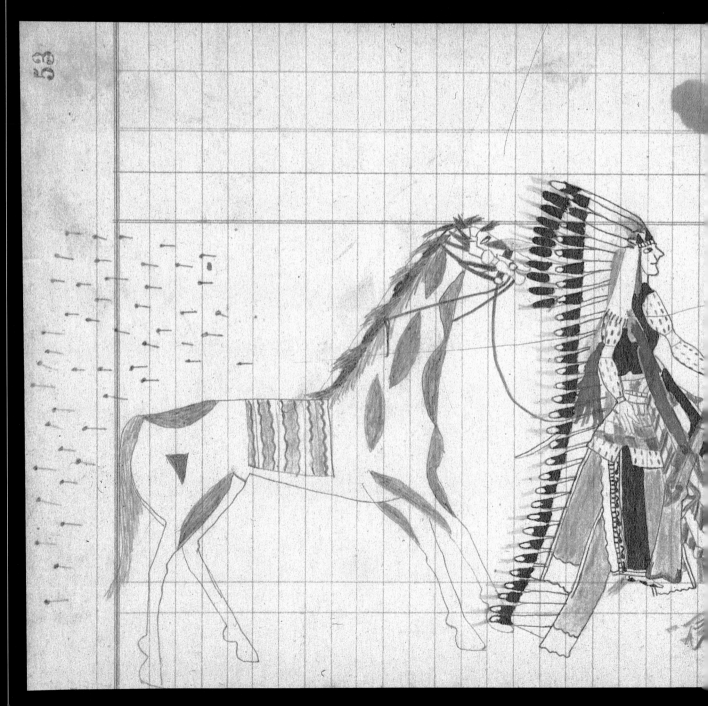

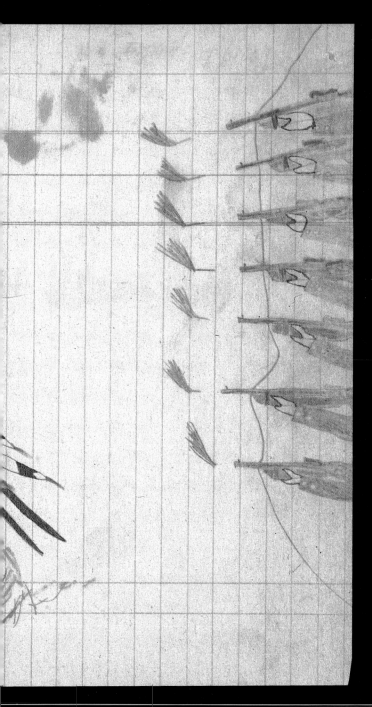

The war for the Great Plains, one of the epic tragedies of American history, was kindled in the mid-19th century by the intrusion of white migrants on the homelands and hunting grounds of the Indians. Within a few decades, the vast open range west of the Mississippi River was riven by thoroughfares for white emigrants. And by 1890, the region's original inhabitants—tribes whose territories stretched from the Canadian wilderness to the deserts of northern Mexico—had suffered total military defeat and a devastating transformation from free hunters and warriors to impoverished wards of the burgeoning nation.

During that era and in the years immediately following, the Indian chroniclers of this cataclysm recorded its events in pictographs, which were collectively called ledger drawings because many were rendered on the pages of ledger books. Those reproduced here, by Northern Cheyenne artists, depict tribal personalities and events, including the Plains wars' most storied engagement, the annihilation by allied Sioux and Cheyenne forces of Lieutenant Colonel George Armstrong Custer's men at the Battle of the Little Bighorn.

The drawings also document the enduring pride of Indian warriors, who regarded combat as among the noblest of life's endeavors. In their battles with traditional enemies, the supreme honor for many Plains Indians was to count coup—to boldly touch an enemy as a way of capturing his spirit. Such ritualized feats persisted, even when warriors clashed with white settlers. As the years passed and Indians were subjected to the perpetual punishing blows of total war, they continued to fight with fervor and celebrate their exploits.

◄

Standing his ground despite his wounds, the Cheyenne hero Yellow Nose unflinchingly faces a hail of white soldiers' bullets. In accordance with Plains tradition, warriors sometimes rode out to face soldiers alone, testing the power of their personal medicine against the weapons of their enemies.

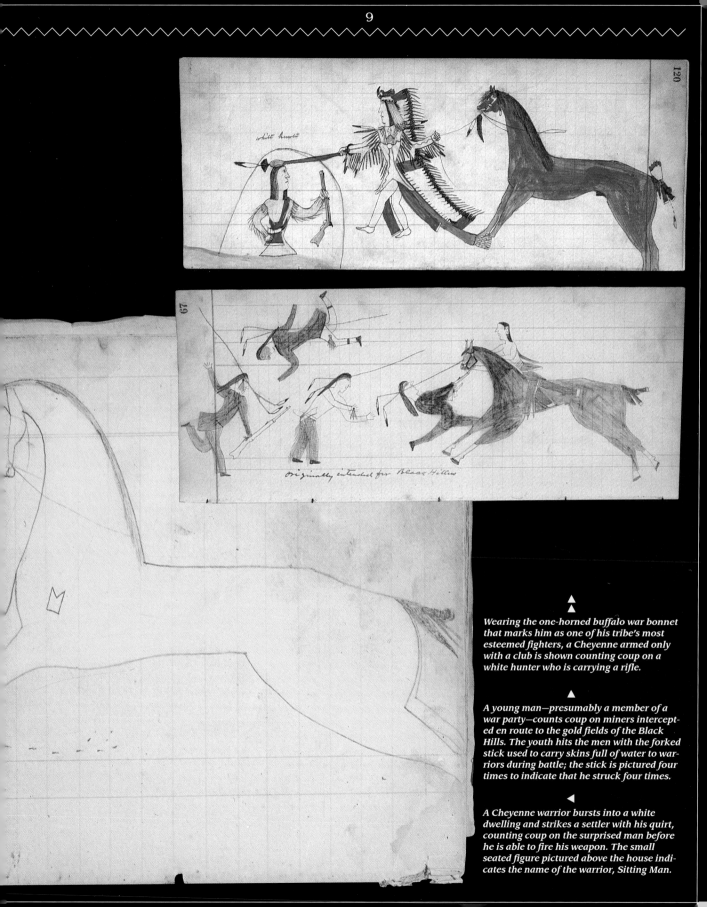

Wearing the one-horned buffalo war bonnet that marks him as one of his tribe's most esteemed fighters, a Cheyenne armed only with a club is shown counting coup on a white hunter who is carrying a rifle.

A young man—presumably a member of a war party—counts coup on miners intercepted en route to the gold fields of the Black Hills. The youth hits the men with the forked stick used to carry skins full of water to warriors during battle; the stick is pictured four times to indicate that he struck four times.

A Cheyenne warrior bursts into a white dwelling and strikes a settler with his quirt, counting coup on the surprised man before he is able to fire his weapon. The small seated figure pictured above the house indicates the name of the warrior, Sitting Man.

In the heat of a pitched battle, Yellow Nose rides down a soldier and, without first trying to count coup, skewers his foe with a lance.

Before attempting to escape the rifle fire that cut down his horse, a warrior shows courage under pressure by removing its valued bridle. A heavy toll of horses was one indication of the escalating carnage on the Plains.

WARRIOR VERSUS SOLDIER

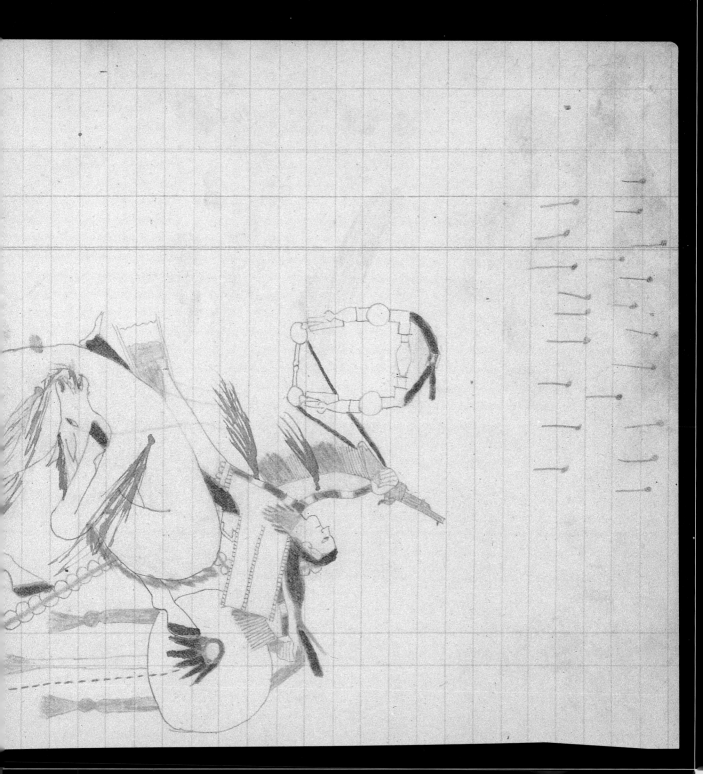

Soldiers chased & killed.

24

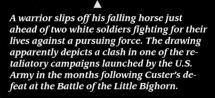

A warrior slips off his falling horse just ahead of two white soldiers fighting for their lives against a pursuing force. The drawing apparently depicts a clash in one of the retaliatory campaigns launched by the U.S. Army in the months following Custer's defeat at the Battle of the Little Bighorn.

In the thick of the fray at the Little Bighorn, Yellow Nose uses a flag captured from the 7th Cavalry to count coup on the doomed men of Custer's command. The celebrated warrior survived the battle and lived into the 1930s as a respected Cheyenne healer.

CLIMACTIC BATTLES

Cheyenne Camp attacked at Powder River
by Soldiers. (Mackenzies)
Fall of 1876

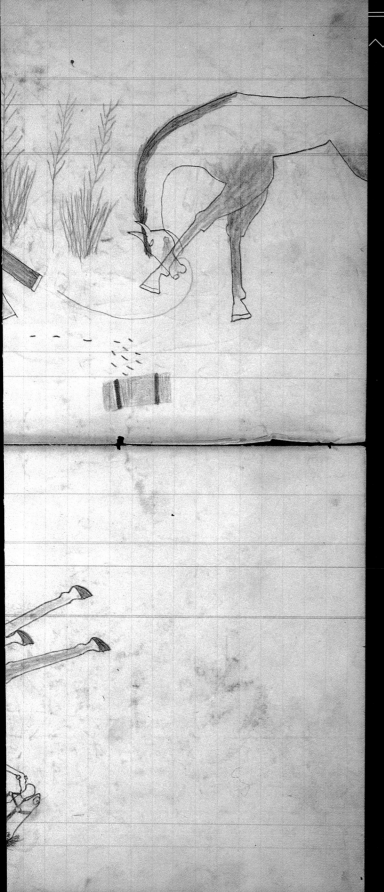

RELENTLESS PURSUIT

In the fall of 1876, Colonel Ranald Mackenzie attacked an encampment of Cheyennes
who had scattered after the fight at the Little
Bighorn. An unusual double ledger drawing
portrays the ensuing action. In the top drawing, three Cheyennes rush from their tipis to
meet Mackenzie's soldiers. The warrior in
the lead wears a one-horned war bonnet and
carries the Thunder Bow, both of which attest to his bravery. The five cavalrymen in
the bottom picture represent the force that
swept into the camp. The trailing rider, with
a red face and long hair, denotes one of the
Indian scouts who aided Mackenzie.

1

THE DAKOTA UPRISING

Little Crow of the Dakota Sioux displays his chief's staff in a photograph taken in 1858 during one of his trips to Washington, D.C., to plead with the government for fairer treatment of his tribe. After long advocating peace with the whites, Little Crow was persuaded to lead the violent uprising by Dakotas in Minnesota that helped spark two decades of conflict on the Plains.

One day in the spring of 1854, a painter of western scenes named John Mix Stanley received a visit at his studio in Washington, D.C., from a man uniquely qualified to judge the authenticity of his work. Stanley had recently returned from the Minnesota Territory, where he had sketched life among the Dakota, or Eastern Sioux— impressions he was now committing to canvas. His visitor on this occasion was none other than the Dakota spokesman Little Crow, whose native village of Kaposia was the subject of two of Stanley's paintings.

Little Crow had come to Washington to confer with government officials about a treaty that would move his people westward from the woodlands near the Mississippi River, where Stanley had encountered them, to a reservation along the Minnesota River. In return, the Indians would receive annuities: regular allotments of cash from the government. A pragmatist who believed that the Dakota had more to gain by accommodating the land-hungry whites than by defying them, Little Crow supported the deal. But he wanted assurances that the government would respect the boundaries of the reservation and meet its financial obligations. And he knew that even with such promises the move would be trying for his people because they would have to abandon Kaposia and other villages.

When Little Crow arrived at Stanley's studio, the artist was finishing up a study of daily life in Kaposia, showing women cleaning hides as men carried canoes down to the river. Little Crow gestured to familiar details in the scene with evident delight. But a second picture drew from him a far different response. That painting portrayed the remains of dead Indians being arrayed on a scaffold outside Kaposia in keeping with Sioux custom, which called for the deceased to be placed close to the sky and its spirits. Little Crow brooded silently over the funeral scene for a while. Then he clasped his hands above his head and walked abruptly from the room.

Those with Little Crow at the time could only guess at his somber thoughts. Perhaps the painting reminded him that moving to the reservation meant forsaking the last resting place of many of his kin. Or perhaps he saw the depiction of this solemn ceremony as an ill omen—a sign that intruders might one day capture the heritage of the Dakota along with

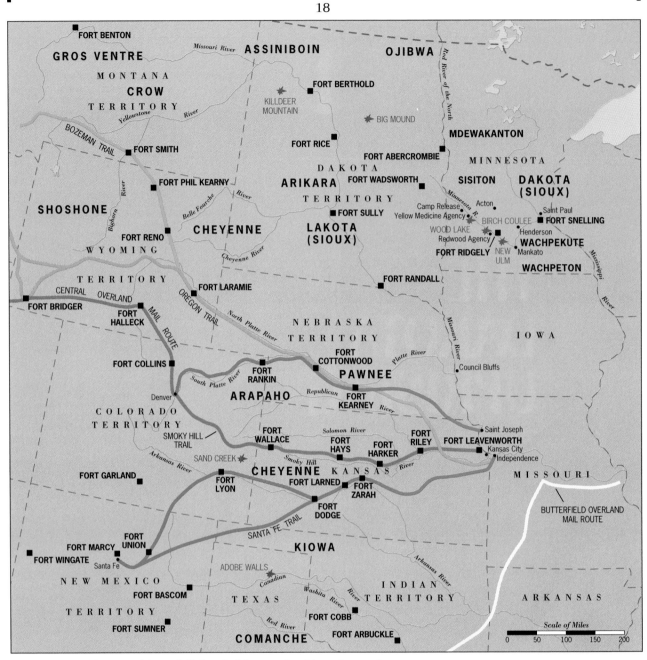

their land and deprive them of all they held sacred. Whites themselves saw something mournful in the work of artists like Stanley, whose efforts to preserve Indian customs on canvas were widely viewed as monuments to a doomed way of life. As one admirer said of Stanley's work: "I consider it the last best offering of this sort which will ever come to us from the wilderness home of this people. Their destiny as a race is sealed. They will soon be lost to our sight forever."

At times Little Crow himself may have harbored such forebodings, but he did not surrender to them. Like other Native American leaders in this era of rapid westward expansion by whites, he was well aware of the material advantages the intruders possessed. But he continued to trust in the spiritual assets of his people—a courage and resolve nourished by their

By the 1860s, the Plains tribes were increasingly subject to encroachment by settlers, miners, and other westering whites. The map shows the Oregon Trail and other routes that were followed by the flood of emigrants as well as the main forts, trading posts, and other early settlements established in the trans-Mississippi West.

ceremonial relationship with higher powers. Ultimately, Little Crow would renounce his cautious ways and lead a bloody campaign against encroaching whites in Minnesota. Underlying that conflict and other such clashes was the conviction of the Indians involved that they stood to lose more than their land if they conceded without a struggle. In the end, the fate they feared most was the erosion of their moral ground—their ancestral pride and faith. To many, it seemed better to fight desperately against the odds than to yield quietly to an enemy who looked on cherished Indian traditions as the last rites of a condemned culture.

The sharp conflicts that erupted between whites and Indians in Minnesota and elsewhere across the West in the 1860s underscored the failure of a policy laid down by the federal government three decades earlier. In 1834 Congress had taken a bold step that seemingly settled the territorial fate of America's Indians. After a history of passing laws detrimental to native peoples, Congress enacted a measure setting aside a vast area as Indian Country. The region was loosely defined as "that part of the United States west of the Mississippi," with the exception of the states of Missouri and Louisiana and the Arkansas Territory. The limits of Indian Country were left vague, for the nation's boundaries with Mexico in the Southwest and Great Britain in the Northwest were as yet ill defined. But the act reserved for Indians much of the expanse known today as the Great Plains.

This was not the first time that officials had set aside a region for native peoples, only to renege. A separate Indian territory had first been proposed at the end of the French and Indian War in 1763. Time and again, lines had been drawn on maps and almost as quickly erased by the tread of white settlers spoiling for land. Indeed, in 1830 Congress had approved the removal of tribes from eastern homelands that they had been guaranteed by treaty. Native peoples had cause to wonder if this new measure would prove any more durable than earlier assurances. Yet never before had the sanctity of Indian Country been spelled out in such detail.

The new law—the last in a series regulating "trade and intercourse with the Indian tribes"—contained numerous provisions to protect the occupants of Indian Country. No white person was supposed to settle or hunt there, introduce liquor, trade without a license, or so much as set foot in Indian Country without permission. Violators were subject to arrest by soldiers from a cordon of military posts extending from Fort Snelling, Minnesota, southward to Fort Jesup, Louisiana. The goal was to establish a permanent frontier between whites and Indians.

For the first time, there was general optimism that this limit on white settlement might hold. It appeared that the appetite for land, which had dispossessed tribe after tribe, might at last be sated. By pushing the nation's western frontier into the fertile Mississippi Valley during the 1820s, Americans had seemingly acquired enough land for all foreseeable needs and attained what one leader called "national completeness." Some congressmen even proposed giving Indian Country self-governing territorial status as a prelude to possible statehood.

Other considerations reinforced this sense of national completeness. According to reports from federally sponsored expeditions, the expanse beyond the Mississippi Valley comprised a forbidding tableau of grasslands, mountain ranges, and canyons inimical to settlement. Major Stephen Long, an army explorer, went so far as to label the region the Great American Desert. To many white Americans, this daunting hinterland was best left to the Indians.

Nevertheless, the boundaries of Indian Country were eroding even as the law establishing it was being enacted. As the Plains Indians themselves could attest, the West was not entirely a desert. Several tribes occupying river valleys beyond the Mississippi derived much of their subsistence from farming, and their land was coveted by settlers. So many whites ventured across the upper Mississippi in the 1830s that Congress soon had to amend its Indian Country act and shift the Indian frontier westward. There were no effective barriers to inhibit traffic in any case, for the army posts were too few to regulate the flow of settlers or traders.

Practical ambitions aside, dreams of empire led some Americans to argue that the task of nation building would not be fulfilled until the Stars and Stripes flew from sea to sea. In 1845 this idea was articulated with missionary fervor by a lawyer and editor named John O'Sullivan, who wrote of "our manifest destiny to overspread and to possess the whole of the continent which Providence has given us for the development of the great experiment of liberty." Under this fresh rallying cry of Manifest Destiny, the nation transformed itself into a continental power with breathtaking speed. In 1845 the United States annexed the Republic of Texas, which earlier had won independence from Mexico. In 1846 it added all of the disputed Oregon country south of the 49th parallel through a diplomatic settlement with Great Britain. And in 1848 a treaty concluding a three-year war with Mexico gave the nation possession of a huge area ex-

Showing the evil effects of the white man's alcohol, a drawing made by an Indian in the 1840s pictures a tribesman (top right) getting a bottle of whiskey from a trader and then (bottom) suffering the consequences—a case of delirium tremens, with shaking and hallucinations. The drawing was preserved by Nicolas Point, a French Jesuit missionary to the Flatheads and other Rocky Mountain tribes.

tending from present-day New Mexico through California. Over the span of a few years, a union that had recently deemed itself "complete" had increased its territory by more than half. The tenuous Indian frontier decreed by Congress had been swept away; henceforth, authorities would strive to control and confine western tribes.

The flurry of expansion brought more than one million square miles under the American flag, along with some 200,000 additional Indians, most of whom lived in lands ceded by Mexico. Long resistant to outside authority, those native peoples were not easily reconciled to American rule. Defiant chieftains such as the Apache leader Cochise made the most of the rugged terrain by striking at isolated bands of civilians or soldiers and retreating to mountain hideouts. But their war parties remained small, and they seldom chose to stand and fight.

It was across the Great Plains that clashes between troops and warriors grew most intense. There, where nature afforded fighting men little

A painting by a settler on the central Texas plains depicts an 1847 Comanche peace council at which the gathered chiefs decided to grant whites a right of way through their territory in exchange for gifts worth $3,000. The pact proved to be a disaster for the Indians, as white homesteaders grabbed more and more land along the route, displacing the Comanche peoples and driving the game from Indian hunting grounds.

cover, even chieftains who sought to adhere to the traditional Indian tactics of stealth and evasiveness were sometimes drawn into fierce battles. Pressed together by the encroaching whites, some tribal bands ultimately combined forces to mount war parties of up to 1,000 men or more—unprecedented aggregations of warriors that were both more susceptible to detection than the raiding parties of earlier times and more capable of inflicting serious punishment on their white foes. At those locations where the two sides met in earnest, the gentle prairie became a killing ground, and the promise of Indian Country lay shattered.

The Plains Indians were not inherently hostile to whites. Most early contacts between the two sides were peaceful and remained so until massive white intrusions imperiled the native way of life. In the early 1800s, white traders and trappers ventured across the prairie in small numbers, seldom encountering resistance. Some traveled the Santa Fe Trail from Independence, Missouri, to New Mexico; others made their way far up the Missouri River to the edge of the Rocky Mountains in Montana. That northern route was especially attractive to fur traders, who sought pelts from Indians in exchange for goods native peoples coveted, such as metal tools, cloth, and firearms, which soon figured prominently in intertribal fighting. Traders were more than willing to provide guns to Indians because they had little fear of attack. Most tribes welcomed trading posts near their territory, as long as the whites dealt fairly with them and stayed close to the forts.

In time, the presence of traders did much to debilitate tribes that trafficked with them. Liquor flowed freely at the posts and undermined native morale as surely as the fiercest of enemies. More insidious still were the diseases whites introduced, ills for which the Indians had yet to develop immunity. One virulent outbreak of smallpox was carried up the Missouri by steamship in 1837. The virus devastated the farming villages of the Mandan along the Missouri, raged on upstream to kill two-thirds of the Blackfeet population, and later traveled south with the Lakota, or Western Sioux, into Pawnee country, reaching as far as the Comanche in Texas.

The opening of the far western frontier in the 1840s brought fresh challenges for the 160,000 or so surviving Plains Indians. To reach California, Oregon, and other lands of opportunity, white Americans began to cross the prairie in droves, forging new pathways. Emigrants to the Northwest blazed the Oregon Trail, which meandered from Independence, Missouri, to the Platte River in present-day Nebraska, then followed the north branch of that river into the Wyoming Territory, where the trail crossed the

Continental Divide. In 1847 Mormons fleeing religious intolerance carved another pathway, which began at Council Bluffs, Iowa, and paralleled the Oregon Trail into Wyoming before turning south toward the Great Salt Lake basin.

Traffic on these trails and their tributaries swelled to a torrent after the discovery of gold in California in 1848. In covered wagons and stagecoaches, on horseback and on foot, fortune seekers flooded west. In 1849 alone, some 55,000 prospectors crossed Indian Country, most of them during a six-week period. And that was just the first in a dizzying succession of mineral strikes that lured men west to mountainous mining camps strung out from New Mexico to Montana.

The endless wagon trains, rutting the young sod in spring and stirring dust in summer, left in their wake trails of misery and death. Cholera rode with the forty-niners and the Oregon-bound emigrants through the Platte Valley, eradicating nearly half of the Pawnees and convincing some Sioux that the disease had been deliberately introduced by white men to rid Indian Country of its rightful inhabitants. No less destructive in the long run was the impact of the traffic on the environment. Parties foraging for fuel consumed precious stands of timber; cattle and horses denuded valleys of their grasses; and white hunters depleted herds of antelope and other game to feed emigrants. Worse still was the havoc visited on that staple of Plains life, the buffalo. Whites not only shot buffalo for food but also disrupted their migration patterns by fouling the trails with the remains of dead draft animals and livestock and other refuse. Said Chief Washakie of Wyoming's Shoshone, "Since the white man has made a road across our land and has killed off our game, we are hungry,

Throngs of Mormon pioneers wait with their wagons to be ferried across the Missouri near Council Bluffs, Iowa, in a painting depicting the height of the Mormon migration to Utah in 1856. In all, about 80,000 Mormon settlers trekked westward to the Salt Lake valley between 1847 and 1869, vastly swelling the traffic through tribal lands.

W. H. Jackson.

and there is nothing for us to eat."

Indian reaction to the mass migrations through their domains varied from tribe to tribe. Ravaged by cholera, the sedentary Pawnee dared not venture far from the Platte Valley in Nebraska to hunt the departed buffalo because of the risk of crossing their old foes, the nomadic Sioux. Many were reduced to stealing food or begging from wagon trains. Some later served as scouts for the army against the Sioux and their allies.

For their part, the wide-ranging Sioux and Cheyenne at first limited themselves to exacting tolls from white travelers who used trails in their regions. As contact increased, however, tempers flared. Whites began threatening Indians and taking shots at them. Warriors, in turn, raided the wagon trains—for revenge, for plunder, or simply for the honors traditionally accorded men of daring. Soon the raiders began to encounter army patrols, dispatched from posts that were sprouting up across Indian Country. By 1854 the army had 52 forts in the West. Few had garrisons of more than 100 men or any real fortifications; most consisted simply of a cluster of rough buildings built near a stream or spring at strategic locations along the trails. No matter how lonely and vulnerable those outposts were, travelers prized them as way stations and visible symbols of protection.

The white soldiers, with their six-shooters, rifles, carbines, and cannon, generally possessed more firepower than their Indian adversaries, whose trade guns were often of inferior quality. In addition, the bluecoats were far better equipped to conduct lengthy campaigns by virtue of their superior organization. The Indians had strengths of their own, however. Unlike the soldiers, most of whom hailed from the East, they were expert at tracking the enemy on the open prairie and exploiting the scarce water sources. Practically from infancy, they had learned the art of war—from superb horsemanship to consummate skills with bow and arrow, lance, tomahawk, and knife. Above all, they had the quickness and stamina to ride rings around their adversaries, who had been trained in conventional warfare and whose "cavalry" often consisted of mule-mounted infantry. "In a campaign against Indians," a veteran commander named Erasmus Keyes remarked, "the front is all around, and the rear is nowhere."

Indian raids on the Oregon Trail became such a threat to emigration that in 1851 the federal government convened a major peace council at Fort Laramie in Wyoming. A former fur trading post, Laramie had been converted into an army fort two years earlier to protect traffic on the trail. The Indian agent in charge of the council was Thomas Fitzpatrick, an old mountain man and fur trader well known to natives of the region, who called him Broken Hand because an exploding rifle had claimed three of his fingers. He organized one of the greatest assemblies of Plains Indians ever. Some 10,000 people of the northern tribes met at Laramie in September—Sioux, Cheyennes, Crows, Arapahos, Gros Ventres, Assiniboins, Arikaras, and Shoshones. Camped in a forest of tipis, the tribes danced and feasted almost every night, dazzled onlookers with their horsemanship, and appeared in force at council meetings, decked out in their "best regalia, pomp, paint, and display of peace," as one witness put it.

Fitzpatrick was compelled to stretch out the council for nearly three weeks because the gifts he planned to offer the peacemakers in keeping with native custom had been mislaid at a Missouri River landing. The errant caravan of presents, worth $50,000, finally arrived, and the tribal chiefs affixed their marks to the Treaty of Fort Laramie. The chiefs agreed to stop harassing travelers on the trails and to allow the government to build more roads and forts in Indian Country. Most significant, the treaty discouraged intertribal conflict by defining the hunting territories of all the groups—a first step toward delineating the reservations to which they would eventually be confined. In return the tribes were to receive combined annuities of $50,000 for 50 years, a term later reduced by the U. S. Senate to 15 years. The chiefs were granted a special honor, one observer reported: "Each was arrayed in a general's uniform, a gilt sword hanging at his side." Afterward, Fitzpatrick conducted a delegation of 11 chiefs to the White House to call on President Millard Fillmore.

Indian leaders who signed the historic Treaty of Fort Laramie in 1851 were awarded a peace medal bearing a portrait of President Millard Fillmore on one side and a friendly meeting between a white man and an Indian on the other.

Indians gather to trade buffalo skins and other furs in the courtyard of Fort William— soon to be renamed Fort Laramie—in an 1837 painting. In September 1851, the Wyoming outpost on the Oregon Trail was the site of a huge council that involved a large number of powerful Plains tribes, whose leaders agreed to a peace treaty.

The Laramie treaty brought a measure of peace to the Oregon Trail. Then, three years after the signing, a trivial incident triggered an explosion. In August 1854, a cow belonging to a Mormon party bound for Utah wandered from the path into a camp near Fort Laramie where Brulé Sioux— one of the seven branches of the Lakota—were awaiting distribution of their annuities. A hungry young Sioux deemed the stray animal fair game and shared its sparse flesh with his friends.

The next day, a brash young lieutenant named John Grattan marched from the fort with 30 men and a pair of cannon. His detachment entered the Indian camp and demanded payment for the animal or the culprit's surrender. The Sioux chief, Conquering Bear, tried to reason with Grattan through the army interpreter, a Frenchman, but the interpreter was an Indian-baiting drunk and hopelessly inept. When the cow slayer failed to emerge, Grattan opened fire with muskets and artillery. Conquering Bear fell mortally wounded, and hundreds of Sioux warriors burst from their hiding places and overwhelmed the soldiers, killing them all and mutilating the bodies. Grattan's corpse, bristling with no fewer than 24 arrows, was so disfigured he had to be identified by his watch.

The so-called Grattan Massacre, together with other incidents, including a raid on a mail coach, prompted a punitive expedition. In the summer of 1855, General William Harney led 600 men up the Platte River, vowing, "By God, I'm for battle—no peace." On Blue Water Creek, east of Laramie, he found the Brulé Sioux who had defied Grattan. Harney divided his forces and caught the Indians as they were leaving camp. Of the 250 men, women, and children in the band, fewer than half escaped; 85 were killed or wounded, and dozens more were taken captive.

The fact that other Sioux bands soon appealed for peace suggested to many officers that such punishment was the way to deal with Indians. Like Harney, dubbed The Butcher by the Sioux, those officers believed in holding an entire band responsible for the misdeeds of a few. Some even pursued a policy of shooting first and asking questions later when they crossed young warriors on the trail. This happened to several parties of Cheyennes, whose hunting grounds bordered the Oregon Trail and other well-trod paths in Nebraska and Colorado. In 1856 clashes near the Platte cost the lives of perhaps a dozen Cheyennes and about as many whites. The following July, a punitive cavalry force under Colonel Edwin Sumner caught up with a large band of Cheyennes on the Solomon River in Kansas. A white-bearded veteran with a booming voice, Sumner was known to his men as Bull Head because a spent musket ball had flattened itself against his skull during the Mexican War. The 300 mounted warriors facing him were confident of their own power to withstand fire: At the urging of their medicine man, they had washed their hands in sacred waters that were supposed to neutralize enemy bullets.

In a line of three squadrons with carbines at the ready, Sumner's command of 300 men swept down into the valley toward the waiting Indians. Then, as the Cheyennes surged forward, sure of victory with their supernatural armor, Sumner—who knew nothing of their ritual preparations—ordered his men to sling their carbines and draw their sabers. With steel flashing, his troops charged at a gallop and dispersed the Cheyennes, who had no holy medicine to counter those glistening blades. The Indians raced back to the river and across, firing some parting shots. Their retreat was so rapid that, in a furious seven-mile pursuit, Sumner's men managed to kill only nine warriors. Among Sumner's 11 casualties was a young lieutenant named J. E. B. Stuart, who survived a Cheyenne pistol ball to win fame as leader of the Confederate cavalry during the Civil War.

Sumner found and burned the village of the Cheyennes, which had been hastily abandoned. Although Cheyenne war parties later retaliated by attacking army supply lines, their anger subsided. By the summer of

1858, they were allowing hundreds of gold seekers to pass unhindered through the region to new mines in the foothills of the Colorado Rockies. "They said they had learned a lesson," reported Indian agent Robert Miller, "that it was useless to contend against the white man."

Despite such apparent successes, the stringent policy championed by General Harney and like-minded commanders had unsettling repercussions. Punitive expeditions placed fresh demands on the army's scarce resources even as the growing tensions that would soon lead to the Civil War threatened to split the country's military forces between the North and the South. Furthermore, in an atmosphere of enmity between the army and the Indians, it was difficult for officers to retain the trust of tribal leaders and to mediate disputes. Such a peacekeeping role for the army had been envisioned by Congress when it established Indian Country, and some commanders still considered it an important part of their mission. Among both whites and Indians, however, calls for conciliation were being lost amid the angry clamor. Soon, men on both sides who had worked to avert conflict on the frontier would find themselves drawn into the fray.

Among the Indian leaders who ultimately joined in hostilities against whites in the West, few made greater concessions before taking that fateful step than the Dakota leader Little Crow. In backing the treaty that moved his people from their homeland near the Mississippi River to a reservation along the Minnesota River, he boldly defied threats by angry Dakota warriors to strike down the first chief who put pen to the treaty. "I am willing to be the first," Little Crow declared. "I believe this treaty will be the best for the Dakotas, and I will sign it, even if a dog kills me before I lay down the goose quill."

Having thrown his prestige behind the treaty, Little Crow traveled to Washington in 1854 to ask officials to guarantee the reservation's boundaries in perpetuity. He returned reassured, but Congress left it to the president to confirm those boundaries by executive decree, and no such decree was forthcoming. Over the next few years, settlers crowded in on the reservation unimpeded. In 1858 officials again approached the Dakota and asked them to yield roughly half the allotted reservation or risk seeing all of it claimed by the newly organized state of Minnesota. When Little Crow protested, he was told that his people were "living on the land they occupy by courtesy of their Great Father." Indians themselves spoke of the president as the Great Father, but here that polite form of address was be-

VIEWS OF CAMP LIFE

In the summer of 1851, an enterprising 23-year-old artist from Baltimore named Frank Blackwell Mayer traveled by railroad, steamboat, stagecoach, and horseback to see the West—and especially to observe and record the signing of historic treaties that forced the Dakota Sioux of Minnesota to cede 24 million acres of their homeland, opening it to white settlement. Fascinated by the Indians and their customs, Mayer lived for a period of time in Dakota villages and was present at the great tribal get-together that attended the treaty signing at the village of Traverse des Sioux on the Mississippi River.

His detailed pencil drawings, four of them shown here and overleaf, capture the feeling of an Indian camp, showing the Dakota in their traditional setting—and living amicably in the company of whites. "Every day produced some novelty and enabled me to fill my sketchbook with many beautiful and interesting hints of savage life," Mayer wrote in the diary he faithfully kept throughout his trip. But like treaty commissioner Luke Lea and other whites, Mayer failed to see that the treaties were forcing the Sioux from their domain for far too small a reward—and that the seeds were being sowed for a tragic outbreak of violence a decade later.

A tipi of buffalo hides stands in front of an airy summer lodge made of poles and bark in a drawing of Chief Little Crow's village of Kaposia. "There is a home feeling about the interior of a tipi," Mayer wrote, noting the pleasure derived from lounging on "a buffalo robe by the light of a smoldering fire." The open scaffolds by the summer lodges, he reported, were used "for drying maize and during hot nights for sleeping."

Little Crow holds a peace pipe in a portrait done by Mayer at Traverse des Sioux, where the first of two treaties with the Dakota were signed in 1851. The chief, Mayer wrote, was "of a very determined and ambitious nature, but withal exceedingly gentle and dignified."

Sioux Evening meal - Traverse des Sioux - July 20. 1851.

Dakotas at Traverse des Sioux enjoy an evening meal, two of them wielding feather fans to ward off what Mayer termed the "multitudes of mosquitoes" that inundated the riverbank encampment. In the evenings, the artist reported, the camp was filled with song, the Indians chanting to the rhythm of drums and rattles, the Americans singing old English airs, and a group of French traders adding songs from Normandy.

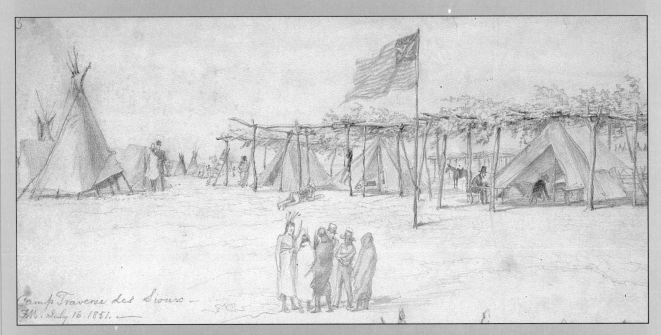

Camp Traverse des Sioux - F.M. July 16. 1851.

Indians and whites chat amiably at the Traverse des Sioux camp where the chiefs' tipis (left) were pitched next to the canvas tents of the treaty commissioners. Impressed by the dignity and grace of the Dakotas, Mayer wrote with enthusiasm in his diary that he had seldom met "in the ranks of civilized life" people who "possessed so much genuine politeness, gentlemanly feeling, and kindliness of manner."

ing twisted to imply that the Dakota were mere dependents of the government and should be grateful for small favors. Incensed, Little Crow declared afterward that he had lost faith in the promises of the Great Father.

In the end, however, he saw no option but to join with other Dakota chiefs in exchanging the requested territory for fresh annuities—much of which went to defray debts that traders on the reservation claimed the Indians owed them. This galling concession cost Little Crow dearly. Young warriors came to doubt his resolve and publicly denounced him. By 1859 he wielded so little influence that he was no longer invited to important tribal conferences with white authorities.

It was a painful time not only for Little Crow but for all Dakotas who were struggling to come to terms with reservation life. Their territory, which once embraced much of southern Minnesota, had been pared down to a 10-mile-wide strip extending along the south bank of the Minnesota River for 150 miles. The 6,000 or so occupants of this reservation were members of four Dakota bands, grouped in pairs around two agencies, where the Indians dealt with traders and received their annuities. Members of Little Crow's large Mdewakanton band along with the tiny Wachpekute band lived downstream near the Lower Agency, while the Wachpeton and Sisiton bands resided around the Upper Agency. Federal officials wanted the Dakota to settle down near the agencies and work the land. For only by inducing native peoples to "cease their wandering ways," declared Commissioner of Indian Affairs Luke Lea, "could the great work of regenerating the Indian race be accomplished."

Regeneration on the reservation did not suit many Dakotas. One major source of resentment was the handling of their annuities. Their grievance had less to do with the relative pittances offered for their lands—little more than five cents an acre under the first treaty and 30 cents under the second—than with a payment system that allowed traders to pocket much if not all of the yearly allowance. Between disbursements, the traders plied the Dakotas with food and other goods on credit, then haunted the pay tables when the annuities arrived and took what they said was due them before the Indians received a penny. There was little to keep traders from inflating their claims, and the Dakotas seethed. One Indian reportedly grabbed his payment of gold coins and swallowed them rather than lose them to a trader. To make matters worse, agents and traders sometimes used their power over the distribution of valuables to gain favors from Indian women—an unseemly departure from the traders' old custom of marrying Dakota women and forging bonds of trust with their kin.

The three chiefs shown here—Shakopee (far left), Mankato, and Big Eagle—served as battle leaders under Chief Little Crow during the Dakota uprising in Minnesota. Mankato was the only chief killed in the fighting, boldly exposing himself to army cannon fire during the Battle of Wood Lake. Big Eagle supported the uprising but was said to have helped a number of white friends escape the attacks.

Such abuses persisted despite protests from some whites. The Episcopal bishop of Minnesota, Henry Benjamin Whipple, went to the White House in 1860 to urge reform of the reservation system. Speaking with President James Buchanan, he declared prophetically that "a nation which sowed robbery would reap a harvest of blood."

Another sore point for many Dakotas was the government's effort to turn them into farmers. Even though the head of each family on the reservation could claim 80 acres of good bottom land, along with plows, seeds, and fencing, fewer than one man in four consented to try farming. In the Dakota culture, tending crops was women's work. For a man to abandon the traditional pursuits of hunting and fishing for farming required a cultural conversion, one that came most easily to those who had strong ties to whites and were ready to emulate them. Such converts cut off their traditional scalp locks—a practice that earned them the nickname Cut Hairs—and abandoned breechcloths for long pants; many embraced Christianity and forsook tipis for houses.

For most Dakotas, the pull of tradition remained strong. These so-called Blanket Sioux shunned white clothes and customs. The men continued to roam for much of the year, foraging on their former territory, where whites considered them interlopers. Such traditionalists derided Indian farmers as Dutchmen—a reference to the German immigrants who had settled near the reservation—and they bristled when Indian agent Thomas Galbraith tried to promote farming by distributing larger annuities to those willing to work the land. To defend their old way of life, militant young Dakotas revived the institution of the soldiers' lodge—a

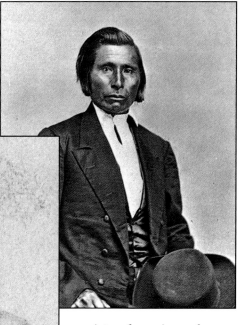

Friendly to the whites, Chiefs Wabasha, Red Iron, and John Other Day, shown left to right, worked to end the uprising. Red Iron opposed the advance of war parties across his territory to raid farms and villages. John Other Day, a Cut Hair who had cropped his long Indian locks and adopted other white customs, helped the settlers—and had his farm destroyed by vengeful tribesmen.

society of warriors who policed communal activities—and pointedly excluded Cut Hairs from membership.

Complaints rose to a crescendo in the summer of 1862. Men of the soldiers' lodges began to talk of war as a way of reuniting their people. They whispered that with so many whites away fighting in the Civil War, the time had come for the Dakota to reclaim their ancestral lands. Even some Cut Hairs were discontented, for crops were poor. Hunters, for their part, could bag little game on land now claimed by white settlers. Many Indians were close to starvation—and their annuities were more than a month late because Congress, preoccupied with the Civil War, had delayed appropriations. Fearing that Congress would reduce the annuities or that men from the soldiers' lodges would seize them when they arrived, traders began denying Indians credit.

Matters came to a head at the Upper Agency on August 4, when some 400 Dakotas broke into the government warehouse and began carrying off sacks of flour. Lieutenant Timothy Sheehan, dispatched to the trouble spot from Fort Ridgely with a column of troops, unlimbered a howitzer and threatened to bombard the warehouse if the looters did not desist. Order was restored, but Sheehan warned his commander at Fort Ridgely, Captain Thomas Marsh, that conflict was inevitable if the Indians went hungry much longer. Agent Galbraith then convened talks that included trader Andrew Myrick and Little Crow—who was regaining influence among the Dakota as tensions rose. Little Crow had urged in the past that all legitimate debts of the traders be honored, and he asked the traders now to credit Indians with food until the annuities arrived. "When men are

General Views of Fort Ridgley 15 miles above New Ulm Minn

hungry," he warned, "they help themselves." Myrick was unmoved. "If they are hungry," he declared scornfully, "let them eat grass."

At the urging of Little Crow and Captain Marsh, who had arrived from Fort Ridgely, Galbraith finally agreed to distribute food from the government's own stockpiles, and the immediate crisis subsided. But reports of Myrick's contemptuous words reverberated like drumbeats across the reservation. Resentments smoldered for more than a week. Then, on Sunday, August 17, four young Dakota men were returning to the reservation from a futile foraging expedition in the Big Woods—ancestral hunting grounds north of the Minnesota River. Close kinsmen, the youths lived in the Mdewakanton village of Rice Creek, a hotbed of militant sentiment. Two of them belonged to the soldiers' lodge there. Some 45 miles from home, empty handed and hungry, they came across a nest of chicken eggs near the white settlement of Acton. According to Big Eagle, a Mdewakanton chief who later recounted the fateful episode, one of the young men then scooped up the eggs.

"Don't take them," warned a companion. "They belong to a white man, and we may get into trouble."

"You are a coward," shot back the first Indian, dashing the eggs to the ground. "You are afraid of the white man. You are afraid to take even an egg from him, though you are half-starved."

"I am not a coward," rejoined the other. "To show you that I am not, I will go to the house and shoot him. Are you brave enough to go with me?"

In this atmosphere of escalating taunts and challenges, the four Indians went to one house, then the next, killing three men, one woman, and a 15-year-old girl before making off with a team of horses.

When they arrived back in Rice Creek that night, they told their story to a gathering of about 100 men at the soldiers' lodge. The men concluded that it was better to declare war on the whites than to see the youths executed and the whole band penalized in other ways. The village headman,

Fort Ridgely, the only military post in south-western Minnesota, became a haven for white refugees during the Dakota uprising. Consisting only of a stone barracks and other detached buildings, it was vulnerable to attack, but its defenders still managed to hold off two furious assaults by the Dakotas.

Devoted friend of the Indians, Episcopal bishop Henry B. Whipple warned before the uprising that the shabby treatment of the Dakota by traders and government agents would inevitably spark violence. In the aftermath of the conflict, he defied the anger of vengeful Minnesotans to defend Indians taken prisoner. Dakotas, in return, gave him an Indian name meaning Straight Tongue.

Red Middle Voice, then led the war party downstream to recruit his nephew, a chief named Little Six. But the warriors needed a spokesman of wider influence than he if they hoped to enlist the support of other bands. Before dawn, they arrived at the home of Little Crow near the Lower Agency and asked him to serve as their leader.

Little Crow faced an agonizing dilemma. Now 52 years old, he was eager to regain the respect of the young men, and he shared the concern of traditionalists that whites were undermining the Indians' spiritual foundations. "A man could not dress and work like a white man," he once told missionaries on the reservation, "and at the same time adhere to the religion of the Dakotas." Nonetheless, he believed in reasoning with authorities. In recent months, he had even shown signs of embracing white customs. He now lived in a frame house and had trimmed his hair to shoulder length. And although he was not an avowed Christian, he had attended services at an Episcopal mission that very morning. Plainly, Little Crow himself was torn by the conflict between the old ways and the new that was rending his tribe.

When the warriors from Rice Creek appealed to him, Little Crow at first suggested they look elsewhere for a leader. But they would not be put off. Little Crow's son Wowinape, who was with him at the time, later said that under the strain of the decision, his face grew haggard and sweat beaded his forehead. Then Red Middle Voice spoke, addressing Little Crow by his Dakota name of Taoyateduta and calling him a coward. Little Crow leaped to his feet, grabbed his accuser's eagle-feather headdress, and hurled it to the ground. "Taoyateduta is not a coward," he cried, "and he is not a fool." In a speech Wowinape recalled as his most eloquent ever, Little Crow reminded the men of his credentials as a warrior: "Behold the scalp locks of your enemies hanging there on his lodgepoles!" It was not cowardice that restrained him but his knowledge that the Dakota were hopelessly outnumbered: "We are only little herds of buffalo left scattered; the great herds that once covered the plains are no more. See!—the white men are like the locusts when they fly so thick that the whole sky is a snowstorm. You may kill one—two—10; yes, as many as the leaves in the forest yonder, and their brothers will not miss them. Kill one—two—10, and 10 times that many will come to kill you."

A photograph taken at the Upper Agency on the eve of the uprising in 1862 shows a Cut Hair man and his son, who have adopted white man's dress, alongside members of their family in more traditional apparel. The same rift between old and new lifestyles is evident in the background, where the poles of a traditional tipi stand near one of the brick houses the government built for Indians who agreed to become farmers.

"Braves, you are little children—you are fools," he concluded sadly. "You will die like the rabbits when the hungry wolves hunt them in the Hard Moon." The young men had appealed to him as their leader, however, and he would not desert them. "Taoyateduta is not a coward," he repeated. "He will die with you."

A short time later, about six o'clock on Monday morning, August 18, Little Crow led a large party of armed and painted warriors to the Lower Agency. Upon reaching their target, the attackers split into small groups and surrounded a dozen or so stores and other structures that stood on a bluff overlooking the river. The first white man to die in the assault was James Lynd, a fluent speaker of the Dakota tongue who had recently completed a book on Sioux lore but who also had the misfortune to be a clerk for the despised trader Andrew Myrick. Minutes later, Myrick himself was shot dead after he jumped from a second-story window and attempted to run for cover. One attacker paused long enough to stuff some prairie grass into Myrick's mouth—a reminder that in the end it was he, and not the Indians, who had to eat grass.

In all, the angry Dakotas killed 20 men and captured 10 women and children. The toll would have been greater had not warriors turned to looting food, clothing, and ammunition from stores and warehouses, allowing townspeople at other locations a chance to escape. Many who did so were aided by sympathetic Indians. Early on, Little Crow himself headed for the Episcopal mission he had visited the day before and offered the Reverend Samuel Hinman a silent warning—a fierce look that made it clear to Hinman his life was at stake. Hinman and his assistant were among 47 residents who fled north across the Minnesota River to safety. Most were shuttled to the far bank in small groups by the ferryboat operator, Hubert Millier, who held to his task selflessly until Dakotas killed him about noon and severed the escape route.

Soon afterward, a column of soldiers reached the ferry landing on the north bank from Fort Ridgely, 12 miles downstream. Their commander, Captain Marsh, had been alerted at midmorning by refugees streaming to the fort from the stricken agency. Marsh had seen action against the Confederates at the first Battle of Bull Run, but he knew little of Indian tactics and underestimated the strength of the opposition. Approaching the landing with 46 untested recruits, he saw an Indian named White Dog—a farmer presumably friendly to whites—gesturing from the far side, about 150 feet away. White Dog assured Marsh's interpreter that everything was all right and urged the troops to cross. No sooner had they filed down to the water's edge than 200 Dakotas sprang from the heavy hazel and willow brush on both sides of the river and began firing. Nearly a dozen soldiers fell in the first volley. Marsh and the others scrambled into a thicket and crept downstream until they reached a point where all appeared quiet on the south bank. The captain then tried to ford the river with some of his men, but he drowned in the attempt, leaving the recruits to fend for themselves. Only half the contingent made it back to the fort alive.

The ease with which Marsh's troops had been routed buoyed the spirits of the Dakota warriors, who had lost just one man in the attack. Around the Lower Agency, many traditionalists now volunteered to fight, and more than a few Cut Hairs were pressured into swapping their pants for breechcloths and taking part.

At the Upper Agency, Sisitons and Wachpetons learned of the attack about midday and spent the afternoon debating whether to join in the conflict. Among those opposing violence was John Other Day, a 42-year-old Wachpeton farmer who had married a white woman and embraced Christianity. Although the council reached no consensus, Other Day feared there would soon be bloodshed. That evening, he quietly rounded

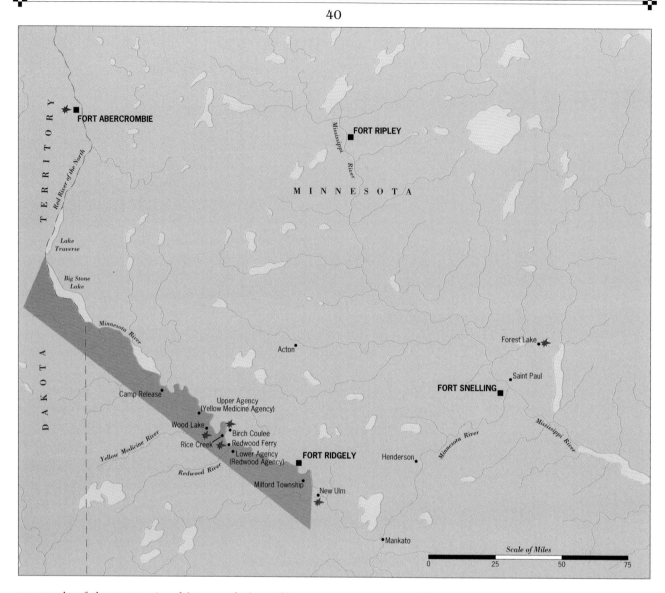

up much of the agency's white population—62 men, women, and children—and escorted them to the warehouse, where he and four relatives stood guard. Several stores near the warehouse came under attack that night when militant Dakotas received word that warriors at the Lower Agency had slain white soldiers "like sheep." Other Day and his relatives maintained their vigil until dawn; then, while the attackers were busy carrying off booty, they loaded the refugees into wagons and led them across a ford in the river to the north bank, where they escaped harm.

Other white civilians were less fortunate. Beginning on August 18, Dakotas scoured the country around the reservation in armed bands of 10 to 20 men, wreaking havoc across a 1,000-square-mile area and claiming hundreds of lives. Surprise was their main asset. Few of the white settlers in the area were seasoned frontiersmen; many of the Germans and Scandinavians did not even own rifles. The marauders often allayed their suspicions by greeting them as friends and shaking hands all around before falling upon them with muskets, tomahawks, or knives. Sometimes the

The map above shows the Dakota Reservation mandated by the treaties of 1851 and 1858 stretching in a slender ribbon along the south bank of the Minnesota River. Before the treaties, the Dakota had roamed most of southern Minnesota westward from the Mississippi River. The battles fought during the Dakota uprising of 1862 are indicated in red; they began with an isolated assault on a farm at Acton on August 17 and spread to the reservation's two administrative centers, the Upper and Lower Agencies, and to white settlements in the vicinity.

Defenders of the settlement of New Ulm fire at attacking Dakotas from behind a hastily built barricade during the first battle for the town, on August 19, 1862, in a painting done on a barrelhead by a resident named Anton Gag. The head of the German settlement's ragtag militia, Jacob Nix, stoutly proclaimed that New Ulm "was defended and saved by Germans," but reinforcements from nearby towns played a major role in driving off the attackers.

raiders killed entire families; in other cases, they dispatched the men and took the women and children captive and brought them back to Little Crow's burgeoning village near the Lower Agency, where warriors had raised a traditional cluster of tipis.

The carnage was worst in the areas bordering the reservation. One of the first targets was Milford Township, which lay downstream from the Lower Agency. The settlers there were Germans, scorned by the Dakota as "bad speakers" because of their faulty English and resented for claiming land the Indians once occupied. On the first day of the outbreak, Dakotas killed some 50 Germans on their Milford homesteads. The following day, a party of raiders encountered 13 German families bound for Fort Ridgely and urged them to return home under their protection. Once the families reached their settlement, the Dakotas turned on them, gunning down 25 people and taking the rest captive.

To whites, such massacres—rendered all the more terrible by the frequent mutilation of corpses—were criminal acts unworthy of fighting men. But to the Dakota, they were part of the age-old ordeal of warfare. In their conflict with the Ojibwa to their north, for example, the Dakota—like native peoples elsewhere—had often dispatched war parties to surprise their opponents at home, in the fields, or on the trail. The men who fell prey to such raids were usually killed, while the women and children were sometimes taken captive and adopted. Warriors felt no compulsion to spare women and youngsters, however, for they were enemies, too, and often aided men on the warpath. Tribal custom sanctioned not only the scalping of foes but also decapitation and other forms of disfigurement, which were thought to deprive the enemy of spirit power in the afterlife.

To be sure, not all Dakotas looked on whites as enemies, deserving of the punishment accorded tribal foes. For one thing, intermarriage had blurred the lines between the two camps. People of mixed blood made up about 15 percent of the reservation population. Many of them protected whites during the conflict, and some were held captive along with white women and children. Few people of mixed blood were killed, however, for fear of retaliation by their Dakota kinsmen.

Even full-blooded Indians who joined in the fighting made efforts to spare whites. "Nearly every Indian had a friend he did not want killed," explained Big Eagle, who reluctantly abandoned his opposition to the uprising soon after it began. "Of course he did not care about anybody else's friend." One way to safeguard friends or their kin in captivity was to adopt them—a ritual that often included dressing the prisoners as Indians. Some

Exhausted and frightened settlers fleeing the violence at the Upper Agency pause briefly to rest during their trek across the prairie. The group headed toward Fort Ridgely but, finding it jammed with other refugees, struggled on eastward and found haven in the town of Henderson. So many settlers abandoned their homes that 23 counties in southwest Minnesota were virtually depopulated.

white women owed their lives to former acts of kindness that the warriors recalled. Sarah Wakefield, wife of the physician at the Upper Agency, was protected because of her husband's care for Indians. Helen Carrothers was spared because she had befriended a shaman, Medicine Man. But a neighbor whose husband had called Medicine Man "a crazy old humbug and fraud" saw her two children slain before she herself was burned to death.

One of Little Crow's half brothers, White Spider, was frank about his motive for aiding whites: He wanted insurance against official retribution. When he helped two women escape the attack at the Lower Agency, one offered him her wedding ring. "I don't want your ring," he replied. "Just look at my face and if anything happens, remember it."

The massacres of settlers distressed Little Crow, who hoped to wage the sort of campaign whites understood—a war on the government's troops and agents that would induce the government to settle with the Dakota on favorable terms. Instead, the raids left whites intent on revenge and diverted Indians from a prime target: Fort Ridgely. Little Crow and several other chiefs recognized that the fort, known to them as the Soldiers' House, was ripe for picking. A cluster of buildings with no stockade, it was swollen with more than 250 refugees, few of whom were equipped to fight. After the loss of Captain Marsh and half of his column on August 18, the fort was held by perhaps two dozen able-bodied soldiers commanded by a 19-year-old lieutenant, Thomas Gere. Among the booty waiting to be seized at the fort were food, blankets, a half-dozen cannon, and, unbeknown to the Dakota, $71,000 in gold—their long-awaited annuities, which had arrived the day fighting broke out, too late to do any good. More important, Ridgely was the only army post in the Minnesota Valley west of that river's confluence with the Mississippi. "The fort was the door to the valley as far as to Saint Paul," Big Eagle said later, "and if we got through the door, nothing could stop us this side of the Mississippi."

Little Crow first attempted to organize an attack on Fort Ridgely on August 19, but the young warriors of the Rice Creek soldiers' lodge who were accompanying him had their eyes on a different prize: the settlement of New Ulm, 16 miles farther downstream. The largest town near the reservation, New Ulm had some 900 residents. Ignoring Little Crow's advice, the warriors attacked the settlement in haphazard fashion and were checked by stiff opposition from the armed citizenry and a smothering afternoon rainstorm. Back at camp that night, they were berated by Little Crow, who urged the Dakotas to "make war after the manner of white men." This time, the young men heeded him.

On Wednesday morning, August 20, Little Crow mounted his horse and led 400 warriors against the Soldiers' House, where the defenders had just strengthened their hold. In the past day, Lieutenant Sheehan—who had quelled the disturbance at the Upper Agency earlier in the month—had arrived at the post to take command from young Gere, bringing with him reinforcements. Fort Ridgely now counted 180 defenders.

Assaulting a large, well-armed force of white men on their chosen ground was something none of the Dakotas had ever attempted. In a battle plan designed to adapt the traditional raiders' tactics of deception to such novel circumstances, Little Crow and his band set out to create a diversion to the west, while the main body of Indians, led by other chiefs, closed in around the far side of the fort, using ravines there for cover. The absence of a command structure among the Indians made tactical coordination difficult, however. Little Crow was recognized by the warriors as the leader in councils. But once the battle began, the various war chiefs acted on their own authority, and the men following them were free to improvise. "After leaving Little Crow, we paid no attention to the chiefs," admitted one of the warriors, Lightning Blanket. "We did not fight like white men, with one officer; we all shot as we pleased."

Nonetheless, the Dakotas attacked with fervor. At the height of the battle, they managed to drive their opponents from breastworks on the northeastern perimeter of the fort and occupy several outbuildings. Sheehan responded with well-placed artillery fire—an ordeal the Dakotas had never experienced and could not long endure. By evening, they had fallen back, cursing the exploding shells as "rotten balls."

Undeterred, Little Crow and his fellow chiefs returned to the fort two days later for what Big Eagle labeled "a grand affair." Nearly 400 Sisiton and Wachpeton warriors had arrived to double the size of the attacking force. The Dakotas were so confident of victory that they brought up a train of empty wagons to receive the munitions, food, and other booty. To get within musket range without being spotted, the Indians fastened prairie grass and flowers in their headbands as camouflage and crept up the ravines. Then they attacked with a shrill chorus of war cries that chilled the defenders to the bone.

After that first brave rush, things went awry for the Dakotas. Withering fire from soldiers crouching behind doorways, window sills, and barricades stopped them short. Warriors set fire to their arrows in the hope of igniting the buildings, but a recent rain dampened the effect. One group of attackers got inside the stables and sutler's store, only to be blasted out by the fort's artillery. Rallying, the Dakotas mounted a fresh assault in the afternoon, pressing forward around the burning stables and the store until federal troops manning a 12-pound gun and a 24-pounder hit them with double charges of canister—tin cases loaded with tiny lead balls. That lethal spray of hot metal, dreaded even by hardened army veterans, terrorized the Dakotas and sent them reeling. After six hard hours of fighting, they loaded their wounded in the waiting wagons and headed home.

This fresh setback left the young warriors hungrier than ever for glory and spoils, and they set their sights again on New Ulm. Since the first abortive attack there on August 19, the civilian defense force had been bolstered by the arrival of newly formed militia units from as far away as Saint Paul. Bereft of big guns, the 300 volunteers were armed variously

with firearms, clubs, and pitchforks. Descending on New Ulm early on Saturday, August 23, the Dakotas created a diversion by kindling fires on the north bank of the Minnesota—across from New Ulm in the direction of Fort Ridgely. A reconnaissance party of 75 men left the town and forded the river to investigate, only to be cut off from the action that followed. Soon the real threat emerged on the south bank—a force of about 650 warriors, some mounted and others on foot, poised on a terrace overlooking the town.

The commander of the settlement's defenders, Charles Flandrau, a 35-year-old state supreme court justice and former Indian agent, witnessed the ensuing attack from the outskirts of New Ulm. "Their advance upon the sloping prairie in the bright sunlight was a very fine spectacle," he wrote later. "When within about one mile and a half of us, the mass began to expand like a fan and increase in the velocity of its approach, and continued this movement until within about a double rifle shot, when it had covered our entire front. Then the savages uttered a terrific yell and came down upon us like the wind."

The defenders quickly gave ground, retreating toward the core of the village. There, in a six-block area behind barricades, huddled more than 1,000 women, children, and other noncombatants, including many recent refugees from the countryside. Determined to shield them, some of the defenders manned the barricades while others challenged the oncoming Dakotas in the streets beyond. Fighting raged from house to house. Both sides deliberately set fire to the wooden structures in different sectors—the Indians to advance from windward under cover of smoke and flames, the settlers to deny them places of concealment. About three o'clock that afternoon, some 60 Indians gathered in a burned-out building near the river for an assault on the barricades. An equal number of desperate defenders uttered their own war cries and charged, scattering the startled Dakotas and ending their hope of capturing the settlement.

Apparently overwhelmed by waves of attacking Dakotas, defenders of New Ulm rally around their commander, bearded, sword-waving Judge Charles Flandrau at right, during the second battle for the village on August 23. The defenders held their ground, but New Ulm was ravaged, with almost 200 buildings reduced to ashes. One of the Dakotas left behind the war club shown at top left.

Nonetheless, the daylong battle had crippled New Ulm. The defenders counted 34 dead and 60 wounded; they could only guess at Indian losses, for the Dakotas made every effort to keep their casualties out of enemy hands. All but 25 of the town's 215 structures lay in ashes. Fearing an outbreak of disease among those who had been crowded in cellars for five days "like sheep in a cattle car," Flandrau ordered the evacuation of New Ulm. On August 25, more than 1,000 civilians and soldiers made the 30-mile journey eastward to safety at Mankato.

The Dakotas were in no position to contest Flandrau's flight. In Little Crow's words, they had waged war "after the manner of white men," braving the shocks of a strange and punishing brand of combat. But they had little to show for it, and now the forces of retribution that Little Crow had feared were approaching from the southeast. Scouts reported that a long column of soldiers was heading up the Minnesota from Saint Paul. The warriors decided to withdraw and seek refuge beyond the Upper Agency, moving with their kin and more than 200 captives in a procession of coaches, peddlers' wagons, and other plundered vehicles.

The commander of the approaching troops was a newly commissioned colonel in the state militia, Henry Hastings Sibley, who was all too familiar to the Dakotas. A former fur trader, Sibley had once been married to a Dakota woman. But any goodwill he accrued through that alliance had since been squandered. In 1858 he had claimed nearly one-third of the payment of $475,000 pledged to the Dakota by treaty on the pretext that they had earlier been overpaid for their furs.

Sibley knew the Dakota people well, but he had never waged war on them or anyone else. Charged by the governor with suppressing the rebellion, as whites referred to it, he worried about the battle readiness of his green troops and feared that the Indians outnumbered them. He moved from Saint Paul with such deliberateness that some Minnesotans suspected that no settlers would be left alive in the western part of the state by the time he got there. One newspaper branded him "the state undertaker with his company of gravediggers." Dakota warriors had completed their withdrawal up the valley by the time he reached Fort Ridgely on August 28 with more than 1,400 men, including elements of the 6th and 7th Minnesota Regiments and mounted volunteers.

While Sibley bided his time, the Dakotas argued among themselves. Some Wachpetons and Sisitons who had fought at Fort Ridgely and New Ulm had since become discouraged and decamped, while others who had refused to join in the fighting were openly denouncing the war chiefs. One dissident warned that "no one who fights against the white people ever becomes rich, or remains two days in one place." At the warriors' new bivouac, mass councils of up to 1,000 Dakotas debated the fate of the captives and the future of the cause. By month's end, two factions had formed and were occupying separate camps close to each other—so-called friendlies, who wanted to release the captives and appease Sibley, and hostiles, who vowed to keep up the fight. Little Crow was sympathetic to the friendlies but remained committed to the defiant warriors who had enlisted his support. On the night of August 31, he and other hostile leaders met in a circle under the stars and pledged to continue the fight.

The following day, September 1, Little Crow led a party of more than 100 Dakotas northward into the Big Woods, where a few white settlements remained intact and were organizing a defense. After two days on the trail, Little Crow's warriors ambushed a local militia company, killing six men and wounding at least 15, then went on to burn and loot the towns of Henderson and Forest City. Meanwhile, a larger party of more than 300 Dakotas led by Big Eagle and two fellow war chiefs, Gray Bird and Mankato, had moved downriver to retrieve possessions left behind at their villages and hunt for targets of opportunity—a foray that put them on a collision course with Sibley's force. Anticipating no such opposition, Sibley had dispatched 150 men from his camp at Fort Ridgely to dispose of the dead around the Lower Agency. Commanded by Joseph Brown—a former Indian agent whose captive wife was under Little Crow's protection—they interred more than 80 victims on September 1. Then they camped for the night at a spot across the river from the agency that was soon to become a fresh burial ground—a deep ravine called Birch Coulee.

During the night, the Dakotas heading downriver approached Birch Coulee. Finding the area occupied, they quietly surrounded Brown's force

A PANORAMA OF CONFLICT

The Dakota conflict had barely ended when a sign painter in Rochester, Minnesota, by the name of John Stevens created a panorama depicting some of the most dramatic and violent episodes of the outbreak. The painter himself had not witnessed the fighting and based his scenes entirely on the lurid and often misleading accounts of others. Still, his panels, executed on a huge roll of canvas, convey a vivid sense of the confusion and terror that were produced by the uprising.

Stevens's disturbing picture

show toured widely in the West. Unrolling the canvas to show one horrifying scene after another, the narrator decried the "bloodthirstiness of the savages." The unfortunate effect was to feed the fears of white settlers everywhere.

The stylized waterfall at left, presumably symbolizing the idyllic beauty of Minnesota prior to the Sioux uprising, provided a suitably theatrical opening panel for Stevens's show. Below, a group of Dakotas, bent on destruction elsewhere, wave to a white settler they apparently consider a friend.

An Indian shoots farmer Andrew Koch in the back while others ransack the farmhouse and ride into a nearby field to capture Koch's wife. The Dakotas in fact killed Koch, but spared Mrs. Koch, who set off through a swamp bordering Lake Shetek (background) to warn neighboring farm families that the Indians had murdered her husband and that they too should expect the worst.

Bravely trying to save a wagonload of women and children from pursuing Indians, a farmer's wife named Lavina Eastlick whips on a pair of horses with a tree branch, while her husband and other men run alongside. The swift-riding Indian horsemen easily overtook the wagon; in the ensuing fight, Lavina Eastlick was wounded and several others, including her husband, were killed.

Two of the many women taken captive by the Dakotas, a Mrs. Smith (far right) and her daughter Julia, are shot by an Indian at close range, a single bullet killing them both. It was reported that the rifle was first raised against the older woman, and Julia threw herself in the line of fire in a vain attempt to save her mother.

A white woman seated at far right, dressed in the artist's fanciful notion of an Indian princess's garb, watches while a group of Dakota warriors perform a victory dance around a fire and another Indian (foreground) writhes on the ground, mimicking victims of the uprising. Many women captives were forced to dress in Indian robes and witness Dakota rituals.

The climax of Stevens's panorama shows
ranks of soldiers and a crowd of civilians
surrounding the huge scaffold at Mankato,
Minnesota, where 38 condemned Dakotas
swing from their ropes after having been
hanged simultaneously on December 26,
1862. The hanging was touted as the largest
mass execution in United States history.

and attacked at dawn with a mixed arsenal of weapons that included double-barreled shotguns. "The white men stood up and exposed themselves at first," Big Eagle recalled, "but at last they learned to keep quiet." Huddled behind overturned wagons, dead horses, and crude breastworks of sod, the defenders languished from thirst while their opponents took turns crawling down to the stream for sips of water. Many Dakotas even had a chance to appease their hunger. "Our women crossed the river and came up near the bluff and cooked for us," Big Eagle explained. "We could go back and eat and then return to the fight."

That afternoon, alerted by the din of battle upriver, a relief detachment of 240 men limbered up two cannon and marched out of Fort Ridgely, only to be stopped short by a small group of Dakotas led by Mankato, who demonstrated so heartily that they fooled the soldiers into thinking they were outnumbered. Mankato's men returned to Birch Coulee laughing "at the way they had deceived the white men," Big Eagle recalled. Colonel Sibley arrived the next morning with his main force to lift the siege after 31 hours. Strewn among the carcasses of 87 horses—every mount but one— were 13 dead soldiers and 47 wounded.

The devastation at Birch Coulee impressed on Sibley the fact that the Dakotas were willing to confront his men and fight "like devils," as he put it. Turning to diplomacy, he wedged a written message for Little Crow in the fork of a stick he found on the battlefield, asking the Dakota if he had "any proposition to make." Little Crow replied through a mixed-blood messenger, reciting past grievances, including the tardy annuities. There followed a further exchange of notes concerning the captives held by the Dakotas. Sibley insisted that Little Crow return them unconditionally, declaring, "and I will talk with you then like a man." In his last message to Sibley on September 12, Little Crow assured him that the captives were being treated well and added, "I want to know from you as a friend what way that I can make peace for my people."

By this time, however, Dakotas in the friendly camp were making their own overtures to Sibley, and he saw no reason to negotiate with Little Crow when obliging Indians were promising to secure the captives and hand them over. Indeed, some peace advocates were already defying threats from hostiles and prevailing on Dakotas who had charge of captives to release them to the friendly camp. Little Crow and his fellow hostiles knew that they had to defeat Sibley soon or lose out to the friendlies. On September 21, Sibley offered them their chance. Cautiously lumbering up the valley toward the new Indian camps with more than 1,600 men, he

stopped that evening a few miles south of the Upper Agency, near Wood Lake. When scouts brought the hostiles word of Sibley's approach, they mustered about 700 warriors and marched the following day for Wood Lake. Only about half of those men were intent on the task, however; the rest were pressured into it or went along in the hope of somehow averting an attack they opposed.

Meeting with other war leaders in council on a bluff near Wood Lake, Little Crow proposed that they surround the encampment and attack that night while the whites slept. Sibley's raw force was vulnerable to such a stratagem, but Little Crow's plan was opposed by chiefs whose true allegiance lay with the friendlies, who denounced the proposed night attack as cowardly. Instead, the Dakotas decided to wait until daylight and ambush Sibley's column as it marched to the northwest.

The presence of warriors uncommitted to the cause was handicap enough for the Dakotas. But as it happened, their ambush was triggered prematurely, and they lost the advantage of surprise. Early on the morning of September 23, a dozen soldiers in four wagons drove out of Sibley's camp and headed toward the Upper Agency to forage amid abandoned gardens there. One of the wagons rolled through the tall grass toward several Dakotas lying in wait. Rather than risk being run over, the Indians rose up and fired, and the battle was joined. With most of his men safely in camp, Sibley was able to hold the Dakotas at bay with cannon fire and sal-

Guarded by soldiers, Dakotas taken prisoner after the uprising sit hunched under blankets outside a log cabin at the Lower Agency. The building was used as a courtroom for about half the hurried trials, which resulted in death sentences for 307 Indians. After reviewing the cases, President Lincoln commuted most of the sentences, condemning only those who had been found guilty of grave crimes against civilians. At right are the three sheets of White House stationery on which Lincoln himself wrote out the case numbers and names of those to be executed.

lies by his infantrymen. Many Indians fired at long range, while others were so far from the foe—or so demoralized—that they never got off a shot. After two hours of fruitless struggle, the Dakotas departed, taking with them the body of the revered Mankato, who had been felled by a nearly spent cannonball. At least 14 other Indian dead remained in enemy hands and were scalped by white soldiers—much to the dismay of Sibley, who said he expected more from "civilized and Christian men."

Wood Lake marked the end of the conflict. The warriors had lost both the battle and their bargaining chips. Returning to camp, they found that friendlies had taken nearly all the captives and were ready to defend them. Some warriors wanted to fight, but Little Crow dissuaded them. The next morning, he bid the camp a bitter farewell. "Seven hundred of our best war-

riors were whipped yesterday by the whites," he said. "I cannot account for the disgraceful defeat. It must be the work of traitors in our midst." Then, with perhaps 200 men and their families, he started for the Dakota Territory—as whites designated the area west of Minnesota. There, he said, his people would "scatter out over the plains, like buffalo and wolves."

The friendlies and discouraged hostiles who stayed behind raised white flags and awaited Sibley's army, which arrived two days later with colors flying. Dubbing the place Camp Release, Sibley took charge of the captives—107 whites and 162 mixed-bloods—and accepted the surrender of the first of nearly 2,000 Dakotas whom he ultimately detained. He then appointed a five-man military tribunal to exact retribution for the conflict's 500 or so white victims, four-fifths of them civilians. The judges wasted no time. They handled as many as 40 cases a day, devoting as lit-

Haze shrouds scores of tipis cramped within a stockade at Fort Snelling, outside Saint Paul, where about 1,700 Dakotas—many of whom had had nothing to do with the uprising—were held prisoner. A number of them died during the harsh winter of 1862-1863; survivors were eventually sent to a distant reservation in what is now South Dakota. As late as 1864, Fort Snelling served as a jail for Dakotas, among them the group of six warriors (inset) that includes Little Crow's son Wowinape (second from right).

tle as five minutes to some. No attorneys or witnesses were allowed for the defense. While some Dakotas were convicted for offenses such as murder or rape, many of those found guilty had merely been present or had fired a weapon during one of the battles. Of 392 men tried, 307 were sentenced to death by hanging.

Episcopal bishop Henry Benjamin Whipple, the longtime critic of the government's reservation policies, appealed the sentences to President Abraham Lincoln. "Talked with me about the rascality of this Indian business until I felt it down to my boots," was how Lincoln put it. Lincoln ordered a review of the trial transcripts by two of his lawyers. In his own handwriting, he later reduced the roster of condemned to 39 men—two of them convicted of assaulting women; the rest of killing civilians.

On the day after Christmas, 38 men—one had received a last-minute reprieve—marched to a common gallows in the town of Mankato. In the end, the condemned observed their own ritual amid the grim ceremony. Standing side by side on the drop that would soon give way beneath their feet, they chanted the "Hi-yi-yi!" of their Sioux death songs and tried to link their bound hands, man to man. "Their bodies swayed to and fro," one witness reported, "and their every limb seemed to be keeping time. The drop trembled and shook as if all were dancing."

William Duley, a settler who had lost his family to Dakotas, came forward to cut the rope and release the drop. Afterward, officials discovered that one man had been executed by mistake—an Indian named Chaska who had rescued the doctor's wife, Sarah Wakefield. The bodies were buried in a shallow grave near the Minnesota River and dug up that very night by doctors who wanted the skeletons for anatomy lessons.

Other punishment awaited the surviving Dakotas. Those with reduced sentences, including Big Eagle, were imprisoned in Iowa, where nearly half died of disease. Minnesota authorities seized the Dakota Reservation and halted annuity payments for four years, awarding the money to white victims of the uprising. Some 1,300 residents—among them many of the friendlies—were banished to Crow Creek Reservation in the Dakota Territory. The land there was so barren and the water so foul that hundreds of Dakotas perished during the first winter. Three years later, the survivors were sent to another reservation in Nebraska; some eventually returned to Minnesota, where their descendants live today.

This Minnesota state treasurer's check for $500 was awarded to farmer Nathan Lamson as bounty for the killing of Chief Little Crow. With the assistance of his son Chauncey, Lamson shot Little Crow while the chief, having returned to Minnesota after seeking refuge elsewhere, was picking berries in a field on July 3, 1863.

Chiefs Shakopee (left) and Medicine Bottle, the last leaders of the Dakota outbreak to be captured, both fled to Canada but were tracked there by agents, drugged, and illegally smuggled back across the Canadian border. After a trial in which they were allowed no effective defense, the two were hanged from a crude gallows at Fort Snelling on November 11, 1864 (top). Told that a last appeal had failed, a resigned Shakopee remarked, "I am no squaw—I can die whenever the white man wishes."

The echoes of the Dakota conflict of 1862 reverberated across the Northern Plains for years to come. Along with Little Crow's band, at least 3,000 other Dakotas fled westward before Sibley took control of the reservation. Many of the refugees were Sisitons and Wachpetons who had shunned the fighting but feared retribution. Federal authorities worried that those exiles would join up with the Yanktonai Sioux already inhabiting the Dakota Territory and with the Lakota farther west. To discourage a wholesale uprising, the army mounted punitive expeditions in 1863 and 1864, but the campaigns only further embittered the Sioux and set the stage for wider conflict.

Little Crow did not live to see the outcome. He spent the winter and spring of 1863 on the Dakota plains trying in vain to form an alliance with other bands of Sioux. Then he returned to Minnesota with a small raiding party, aiming to steal horses for his kin "so that they could be comfortable," his son Wowinape explained, "and then he would go away off." On July 3, he and Wowinape were picking raspberries near the Big Woods when two white farmers, Nathan Lamson and his son Chauncey, spotted them. The Lamsons did not recognize Little Crow, but they knew there was a bounty on Indians and opened fire. Little Crow fired back, then took a fatal shot. Before departing, Wowinape wrapped his father's lifeless body in a blanket and placed new moccasins on his feet for the journey to the next world.

Along with the standard $75 scalp bounty, the Lamsons received a bonus of $500 from the state for ridding Minnesota of Little Crow, who had dared to fight for the land as if it were truly Indian Country. ◆

THE RESERVATION WAY

In a sketch drawn by a young Sioux, an Indian agent doles out supplies from the back of a wagon (below). Agents wielded total power on the reservation, controlling land use, administering tribal funds, and enforcing the law.

In 1850 Commissioner of Indian Affairs Luke Lea outlined to Congress a new federal program for the assimilation of all American Indians "into the great body of our citizen population." This policy would be carried out through agriculture, practiced in enclaves where Indians would be compelled to live until they were transformed into replicas of white farmers. These reservations would include all existing Indian preserves as well as those yet to be marked off for what Lea termed "our wilder tribes."

Within three decades, some 360,000 Indians were consigned to 441 federal preserves across 21 states and territories. Indian agents appointed to run the reservations were responsible for both education and the enforcement of regulations designed to eradicate all elements of Indian culture. The goal was for the Indians to support themselves and settle on individual homesteads, freeing tribally owned "surplus" lands to be sold to white settlers. At that point, the reservation would cease to exist. The Indians, all traces of cultural identity erased, would slip smoothly into the American mainstream.

Many well-meaning whites regarded this policy as both enlightened and humane. But for the nomadic hunters and warriors of the Great Plains, robbed of their freedom and commanded to forswear their language, tribal loyalties, kinship ties, and religious traditions, it proved as cruel and destructive as the military campaigns that had recently been waged against them.

Sioux at South Dakota's Pine Ridge Reservation wait in line to receive their weekly rations. Deprived of the wild game that had once provided their food, some reservation Indians dryly dubbed the U.S. government the "new buffalo."

SUPPLIES FOR THE CORN ROAD

Southern Plains women butcher government issue cattle in the Oklahoma Territory in 1901 (above). Beef rations were typically supplied on the hoof to families or small groups. Mounted men slaughtered the cattle on the open plain, evoking nostalgic echoes of the buffalo hunt.

Reservation dwellers depended on government supplies for survival. Weekly rations of food, clothing, and staples were meant to tide the Indians over until they could grow crops to replace buffalo meat and the goods obtained from trading hides. Kept deliberately meager in the belief that such handouts encouraged idleness, rations were distinct from annuities—money, goods, or services paid to the Indians in exchange for their lands. Annuities frequently took the form of tools, seed, livestock, and help from agency farmers to start the Indians on what was called the Corn Road.

In practice, neither rations nor annuities were sufficient to meet the Indians' needs. "When the goods come, they never fulfill the treaty," reported Struck by the Ree, a Yankton Sioux, in 1865. Supplies were often stolen by corrupt agents or unscrupulous contractors and never reached the Indians at all.

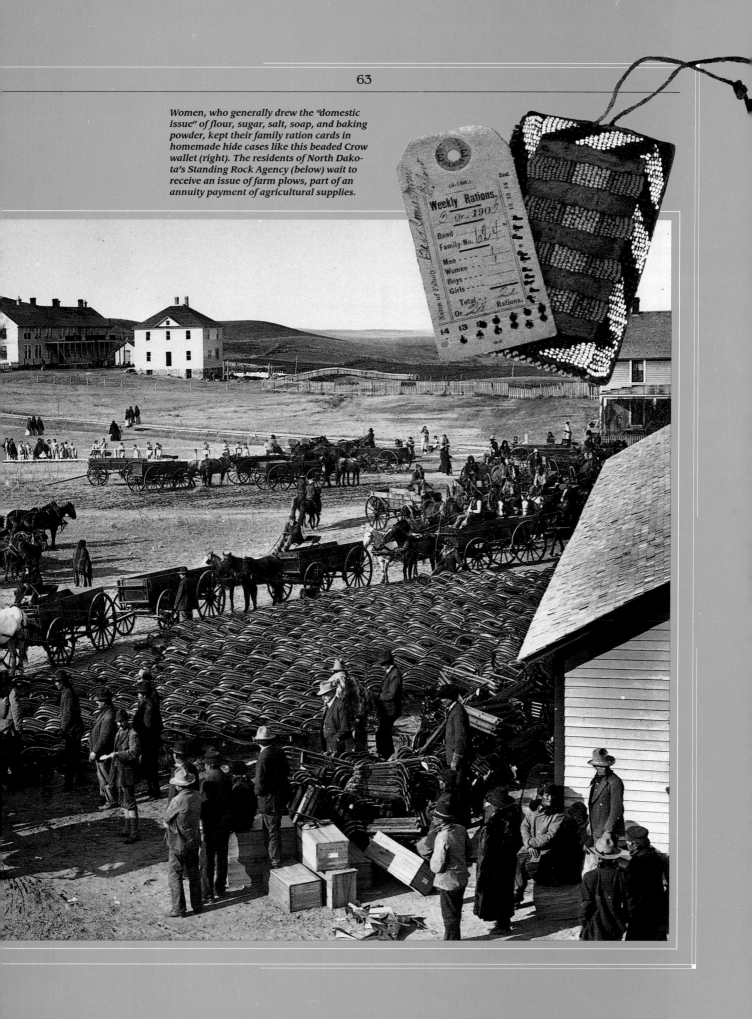

Women, who generally drew the "domestic issue" of flour, sugar, salt, soap, and baking powder, kept their family ration cards in homemade hide cases like this beaded Crow wallet (right). The residents of North Dakota's Standing Rock Agency (below) wait to receive an issue of farm plows, part of an annuity payment of agricultural supplies.

MAKING DO WITH LITTLE

The scheme to transform buffalo hunters into farmers faced formidable obstacles. Plains men traditionally disdained agriculture as women's work. Moreover, the arid climate and poor growing conditions on most Plains reservations doomed the efforts of those who could be persuaded to try farming.

Many Indians eventually had to find employment in order to survive, working on or near their reservations as laborers, loggers, or cowhands. Some parts of the Plains had good grazing land that could support cattle as it once had buffalo, and stock raising became a popular alternative to sodbusting. But cattle required more land than crops, and the government's zeal for installing Indians on individual land allotments and instilling the principles of private property undermined efforts to use open reservation land as a communal cattle range. Few Indians were able to amass sizable herds and compete successfully with white ranchers.

Working to earn extra rations, Blackfeet Indians joined northern Montana logging crews in the early 1890s. A sawmill and slaughterhouse located on the reservation employed other members of the tribe.

Sioux cowboys brand steers on the Rosebud Reservation (left). Their cattle could not be sold or slaughtered without government permission. The animals typically bore both an Indian Department brand, such as the iron at far left, and that of an individual owner.

In 1908 Blackfeet workers excavate a section of Saint Mary's Canal, part of a large-scale project designed to irrigate reservation fields. Paid for by tribal funds, the network of ditches ultimately watered the fields of white farmers who purchased reservation property.

A missionary woman pays a call on a Northern Plains family about 1900. The conversion of Indians to Christianity was an avowed public policy goal, and missionaries were welcomed by reservation officials as teachers and exemplars of civilized conduct for the Indian peoples.

The tipi, sweat lodges, and rack of meat seen drying in the sun beside this Crow family log cabin testify to the reluctance with which reservation Indians relinquished old ways. By the turn of the 20th century, as many as one-third of all Crow Indians still lived in tipis, most of them pitched next to the houses of relatives.

LEARNING NEW HABITS

The white-imposed standards on which Indians were expected to pattern their private lives were as confounding to most of them as the hoe and plow. "We had everything to learn," recalled an Arapaho named Carl Sweezy. "We had to learn to cut our hair short and to wear close-fitting clothes made of dull-colored cloth. It was a long time before we knew what the figures on the face of a clock meant."

Strangest of all, however, were the new dwellings in which they were to live. Frame houses were structures so alien that some Indians, upon seeing them for the first time, thought that the windows had been put in the walls "so that we might look in to see how white people did their work."

Clothed in traditional Indian dress, a Crow family dines at home amidst the trappings of white middle-class prosperity (left). Tableware was a novelty to the majority of Plains Indians; the fork above was whittled from a cow's horn and decorated with a carved-out buffalo head.

A group of young Sioux children gather in front of a mission day school at the Standing Rock Agency in North Dakota. By the 1880s, the small day schools that had been established over the years by evangelical missionaries were incorporated into the federal system and shared a common curriculum.

COMPULSORY SCHOOLING

In a drawing by a Crow youth (below), the cigar-puffing agent of Montana's Crow Reservation and his Indian chief of police compel a reluctant mother to send her daughter to the agency school. Parents who refused to put their children in school were sometimes jailed or denied their rations.

The most intense effort to propel Indians into white society took place in the schoolroom. Compulsory education of Indian children was the key to government's assimilation aims, and by the late 1880s, federal schools were operating on every reservation in the country, part of an education system that also included off-reservation boarding institutions. These schools, which were organized along the rigid lines of military academies, sought to force young Indians to give up what one teacher termed "their wild barbarous things"—a category that included their clothing, their long hair, their language, even their own names. "I believe in immersing the Indians in our civilization," declared Richard Pratt, a prominent Indian educator, "and when we get them under, holding them there until they are thoroughly soaked."

Some children flourished under this drastic regimen. Many more were deeply traumatized. Absenteeism became epidemic. By 1900 only about 15 percent of those who had passed through the system had more than a few years of primary education.

A trio of runaway girls is carted back to the Oklahoma Territory's Seneca Training School in 1901. Homesick boarding school students repeatedly fled to their families, risking harsh punishments that included beatings, confinement, and public humiliation; runaway boys at the Phoenix Indian School were forced to wear girls' clothing.

Pupils sit in orderly rows at their desks in a classroom at the Riverside Indian School, a boarding school in Anadarko, Oklahoma.

Indian students tend the gardens at Santee Normal Training School in Nebraska. Such farms and gardens filled a twofold purpose: training in agricultural skills and defraying school costs by providing food for students and staff.

Children learn to wash clothes at the Riverside School. Educators of Indians expected that their students would return to the reservation and teach their elders the domestic skills they had learned at school.

2

WILDFIRES ON THE PRAIRIE

Decorated with thunderbirds and other sacred symbols, the shield at left was carried by the Cheyenne chief Little Rock during the battle at Washita River in 1868. After Little Rock died in the carnage, his shield was recovered by Lieutenant Colonel George Armstrong Custer, who presented it and the chieftain's scalp to a nature society in Michigan.

Few white men did more to shape the destiny of Plains Indians than William Bent. As the manager of Bent's Fort, a trading post strategically located along the Santa Fe Trail and the Arkansas River near present-day La Junta, Colorado, he transformed the lives of the many Indians who flocked there—primarily Cheyennes and allied Arapahos, who came to exchange buffalo hides and other furs for guns and clothing, tools and cooking utensils, and such enticing items as coffee, sugar, and whiskey. So strong was the lure of trade that it contributed to tribal divisions, with the Southern Cheyenne and Arapaho gravitating toward Bent's Fort while the Northern Cheyenne and Arapaho remained up around the Platte River and forged ties with the Lakota, or Western Sioux.

Even as Bent changed the ways of his Indian clients, however, they had a profound effect on him. Like other shrewd white traders on the Plains, he married an Indian woman—a Cheyenne named Owl Woman, who bore him several children. When Owl Woman died, he followed tribal precedent and wed her sister, Yellow Woman. Bent's children grew up in a setting where Indians were in the overwhelming majority, and they came to identify closely with the Cheyenne. For them as for their father, the problems that afflicted the tribe hit home.

By 1859 the Southern Cheyenne and Arapaho were in a sad state. Like other tribes, they had suffered diseases and disruptions through their dealings with whites, and now they faced a grave threat to their livelihood. The treaty their chiefs had signed at Fort Laramie in 1851 had acknowledged their right to stalk the buffalo grazing east of the Rocky Mountains between the Arkansas and the North Platte Rivers. But that coveted hunting ground was now being crossed by thousands of white prospectors bound for the emerging village of Denver and the new gold fields in the hills beyond. The traffic and debris scared away the buffalo, depriving the Indians of not only meat and hides but also trade goods they had come to rely on.

As federal agent for the Southern Cheyenne and Arapaho, William Bent sought to bring their plight to the attention of his superiors. He determined to write a letter on behalf of the Indians, but a small obstacle intervened—frontier life had left him uncertain as to the rudiments of English composition. "I have bin so long in the Wild Waste," he admitted in one note, "I have almost forgotten how to Spell." With help from sympathetic officials, however, his prose was cleaned up, and the report that reached the U.S. commissioner of Indian affairs was both cogent and forceful.

"A smoldering passion agitates these Indians," Bent wrote, "fomented by the failure of food, the encircling encroachments of the white population, and the exasperating sense of decay." Little could be done to halt intrusions by whites, he conceded, but the government could rescue the two tribes by "withdrawing them from contact" with hostile frontiersmen and settling them on a reservation. Barring that, he concluded, they would soon become the victims of a "desperate war of starvation and extinction."

Bent's proposal—which was endorsed by his superiors and eventually resulted in a reservation for the Southern Cheyenne and Arapaho—was proof that good intentions as well as bad underlay the calamitous federal Indian policies of the day. Although some whites looked on reservations as mere pretexts for removing tribes from coveted land, others regarded them as the only way to prevent conflicts that might result in the annihilation of native peoples. As for the Indians, among those inclined to accept the need for reservations were a number of older chiefs who had lost the combative fervor of their youth and knew how dangerous whites could be when their territorial ambitions were at stake.

The burden of reconciling the Southern Cheyenne to reservation life fell to the influential chief Black Kettle, a former war leader who was now about 50 years old and believed firmly that his tribe could be preserved only through peaceful accommodation with whites. His was an unenviable position, for as Little Crow had learned in Minnesota, the bright promises federal officials made when they established reservations were seldom fulfilled, and the resulting unrest encouraged rebellious young warriors to defy tribal authorities and lash out at nearby whites. Too often, confinement to a reservation simply postponed the bloody showdown that the conciliators feared—and left tribes all the more divided and vulnerable when the fighting erupted.

William Bent had no desire to expose the Indians to such a fate. He wanted to insulate them from clashes with whites, if only to protect his trade and shield his mixed-blood children. Yet the conflict to come would be all the more bitter for his efforts to avoid it. Deeply affected would be his three sons and the obliging Black Kettle—products of an era of patient give-and-take between whites and Indians that was soon to be forsaken.

At Fort Dodge, Kansas, in 1869, soldiers look on from a rooftop as trader William Bent (second from left) sits for a portrait with Southern Arapaho leader Little Raven (left) and his three children. Appointed Indian agent for the Southern Cheyenne and Arapaho in April 1859, Bent worked fervently on their behalf. He resigned in frustration in 1860 but continued to advise Indians in their dealings with the government.

The Colorado gold rush that threatened the hunting grounds of the Cheyenne and Arapaho was part of an irresistible migratory impulse that was driving a wedge through the heart of the Plains. Prior to the Colorado strikes, buffalo herds and the Indian hunting bands pursuing them had ranged largely undisturbed across the Central Plains, an area bounded to the north by the Oregon and Mormon Trails along the Platte and North Platte Rivers and to the south by the Santa Fe Trail along the Arkansas River. Subsequently, however, Denver-bound prospectors forged two new paths between those established routes—one running along the South Platte River from Nebraska down through northeastern Colorado, and another roughly paralleling the Smoky Hill River through central Kansas into southeastern Colorado, where the trail proceeded toward the mining camps along a stream known as Big Sandy Creek, or Sand Creek. Federal authorities undertook first to protect travelers on those new routes and later to secure the Central Plains as a corridor for settlement and for rail lines linking East to West. Through persuasion and force, the government would seek to keep that corridor free of roaming Indians, and a breach would be forged between the tribes to the north and those to the south.

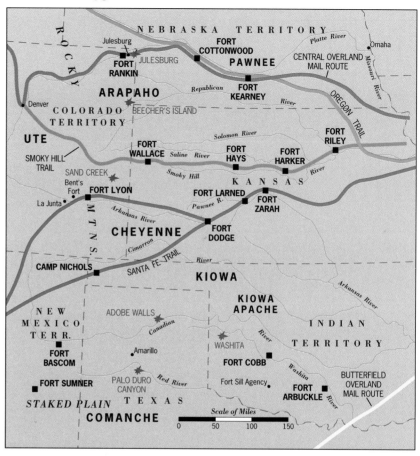

For Black Kettle and his people, this development had far-reaching consequences. For one thing, it meant that their separation from the Northern Cheyenne would eventually become formal and permanent, as would the same division among the Arapaho. In the process, the Southern Cheyenne and Arapaho would be pressed together with tribes whose heritage was quite different from their own—notably the Kiowa and Comanche, whose territory lay south of the Arkansas.

The Cheyenne, like the Arapaho, were an Algonquian-speaking people who had migrated onto the Plains from the northern woodlands. Their 18th-century ancestors had resided in earthen-lodge villages, first along the Minnesota River and later along the Cheyenne River in present-day North Dakota, where they had derived much of their subsistence from farming. Driven westward by rival tribes, the Cheyenne amassed horses and guns and lived as nomadic buffalo hunters, descending in the early 1800s to the Central Plains just east of the Rockies, where they allied themselves with the Arapaho.

The Comanche and Kiowa not only belonged to different language groups than the Cheyenne and Arapaho but also were horse-riding hunter-warriors of longer standing and greater notoriety. Former mountain dwellers, the Comanche swept down from the Rockies on horseback in the early 1700s. Intent on securing hunting grounds, they pushed aside one rival tribe after another before coming to terms in the late 1700s with the formidable Kiowa and a band closely associated with them—the Kiowa Apache. The allied tribes then cast their gaze southward, where their old foes, the Mexicans, were gradually being supplanted by Anglo-Texans, whose burgeoning ranches and villages presented tempting targets. By the time Texas joined the Union in 1845, whites in that state were locked in a vendetta with raiding Comanches and Kiowas.

The Cheyennes and Arapahos who ventured down to trade at Bent's Fort in its early days had problems of their own with the Kiowa and Comanche. After a few sharp setbacks at the hands of those formidable op-

Beginning in the 1850s, strife swept the lower Plains as Indians seeking to hold on to their territory clashed with settlers, who poured into the region by wagon and later by rail. Forts were established to keep the peace, but federal troops eventually found themselves engaged in punitive campaigns aimed at securing the main emigration corridor through Kansas and Colorado by forcing tribes onto reservations to the south.

ponents, however, the Algonquian speakers sought peace: They had ancestral enemies to worry about—notably the Ute to the west and the Pawnee to the east—and the Comanche and Kiowa could not be surpassed when it came to mounted warfare. In 1840 the tribes on either side of the Arkansas buried their differences, and the feuding ceased.

Over the next two decades, as white traffic across the Central Plains increased, the Southern Cheyenne and Arapaho clashed sporadically with the light-skinned intruders. But unlike the Comanche and the Kiowa, for whom raiding Texans was a regular source of pride and sustenance, the Southern Cheyenne and Arapaho were inclined to attack whites more selectively—often in response to some trespass or insult. Unfortunately, that distinction was all but lost on the men flocking to the mining camps around Denver, many of whom had departed for the West impulsively and were daunted by its challenges. They tended to see any act of native defiance as part of a dire Indian conspiracy. With the coming of the Civil War and the departure of Regular Army troops to fight in the East, such fears only increased. The result was the recruitment of a new kind of fighting force, made up of local volunteers whose mission was to shield their communities against the perceived threat by killing Indians, and whose leaders made little effort to distinguish friendly bands from hostile ones.

In February 1861, on the eve of the Civil War, Black Kettle joined with nine other chiefs of the Southern Cheyenne and Arapaho in signing an accord with the whites. Meeting at Fort Wise, near Bent's trading post, the chiefs put their marks to a treaty that consigned the tribes to a small reservation of roughly triangular shape—bounded on the northeast by Sand Creek, on the south by the Arkansas, and on the west by an arbitrary north-south line that lay some distance from the slopes of the Rockies. Prone to drought that left the riverbeds empty, this reservation offered the Indians poor prospects, whether for traditional hunting activities or for the farming they were expected to take up as part of the deal. For 15 annual payments of $30,000—some of which would go to cover such expenses as fencing, housing, and livestock—they were supposed to stop roaming and start planting with the help of government agents. The allotment of 40 acres for every male Indian appeared generous, but the soil was so inferior, even experienced farmers would have been hard pressed to succeed.

The inadequacy of the land was just one factor that undermined the Treaty of Fort Wise. Many of the chiefs who signed did not fully understand the terms and had limited authority over others in their bands. Furthermore, the pact did nothing to resolve the fate of the Northern Cheyenne and Arapaho, although Colorado officials later tried to induce them to acknowledge the treaty and move to the same reservation. In addition, a powerful band related to the Southern Cheyenne were adamantly opposed to the deal. These were the so-called Dog Soldiers, who were unique among Cheyenne warrior societies in that they formed a separate group within the tribe. The Dog Soldiers answered only to their war chiefs, none of whom had signed the treaty. In the future, they would be a thorn in the side of Black Kettle and others who sought to avoid conflict with whites.

For a while, none of this mattered. The Civil War preoccupied Washington, and little was done to enforce the treaty. The Southern Cheyenne and Arapaho soon found their reservation unfit for either hunting or farming and persisted in their itinerant ways, stopping at the former Fort Wise—renamed Fort Lyon in honor of a Union general—long enough to collect their annuities. By and large, they kept the peace, despite provocations from fortune seekers, settlers, and troops. On one occasion, William Bent reported, a soldier from Fort Lyon offered an Arapaho some whiskey in exchange for a "squaw to sleep with." In no mood to honor the request, the Indian took the whiskey and shared it with some of his friends in their lodge, where the soldier later sought out the Arapaho and shot him in the arm. Remarkably, this affront went unanswered.

Had the Indians chosen to, they could have made things hot for the bluecoats. With most troops dispatched to the East for Civil War duty, just 300 soldiers remained by 1862 to defend four posts in western Kansas and eastern Colorado. A Confederate agent named Albert Pike tried to exploit the situation by urging tribes to defy the Federals, but William Bent persuaded the Southern Cheyenne and Arapaho to stay out of this "white man's fight," as he called it. Hostility toward white intruders was greater among the Northern Cheyenne and Arapaho and their Sioux allies. But even they were far from united in opposition.

One influential white man in the area was counting on war with the Indians, however. John Evans, governor of the Colorado territory, believed that the tribes of the region stood in the way of further settlement and his own ambitions: He hoped to be elected United States senator once the territory became a state. Evans first tried to persuade all the Cheyennes and

A lance like the one shown here and a leather sash were the standard regalia of the Dog Soldiers, an elite Cheyenne warrior society whose members adamantly and violently resisted white settlement of Indian lands. A Dog Soldier would pin himself to the battlefield by thrusting his lance through his sash, and stand his ground until he was killed or was released by a fellow society member.

Arapahos in eastern Colorado to move to the one small reservation below Sand Creek—an area plainly inadequate to support the southern factions alone. When that bid failed in 1863, he whipped up fears that the area's far-flung Indian bands planned to join forces and drive whites from the area.

Such a conspiracy appeared unlikely to informed observers such as Major Scott Anthony, the commander of Fort Lyon. Anthony believed that only the Indians to the north posed a serious threat. The tribes in his vicinity, he reported, were unlikely to cause much trouble, dependent as they were on the government for support in the midst of a severe drought that had dried up the Arkansas River for hundreds of miles. Nonetheless, Governor Evans chose to credit such dubious reports as the one he received from a white man named Robert North, who was married to an Arapaho. North claimed to have attended a "big medicine dance," where chiefs told him of an uprising being planned for the spring of 1864 by a grand confederation of Plains tribes, north and south. Evans made much of this tale, for it justified his attempt to force all Indians from the settled areas of Colorado.

Supporting him in that objective was Colonel John Chivington, the commander of territorial forces in Colorado. Like Evans, Chivington nursed political ambitions and saw Indian fighting as a steppingstone. An Ohio-born Methodist minister with an enormous physique and an ego to match, Chivington had won renown as the Fighting Parson in 1862, when he led the 1st Colorado Cavalry Regiment and helped repulse a Confederate invasion force in New Mexico.

In April of 1864, an occasion for Indian fighting arose, and Chivington seized it. In response to reports of livestock thefts by roaming Cheyennes, he dispatched elements of the 1st Colorado. Although the reports were sketchy—the livestock may well have stampeded or simply wandered off—Chivington instructed his men to hunt down the Cheyennes and subdue them. At first, the objective was simply to disarm the Indians, but Chivington soon raised the stakes. Ultimately, one of his field officers asserted, the orders were to "kill Cheyennes whenever and wherever found."

The first clash came on April 12, when Lieutenant Clark Dunn, with 40

In the spring of 1864, Colorado territorial governor John Evans urged Coloradans to take up arms against the Southern Cheyenne and Arapaho. Colorado's military commander, Colonel John Chivington, supported Evans's efforts with unprovoked attacks on friendly as well as hostile Indians. When the Indians retaliated, Evans and Chivington were permitted to raise cavalry volunteers, for whom recruiting posters (right) promised rewards of "plunder from the Indians."

troopers, intercepted a party of Dog Soldiers along the South Platte. The Dog Soldiers had ventured there not to join in a campaign against whites but to help avenge the killing by rival Crow warriors of an esteemed Northern Cheyenne chief. Along the way, they had picked up a few mules belonging to a white rancher, and Dunn set out to retrieve the animals and disarm the Dog Soldiers. The Cheyennes might have been willing to part with the mules, but they were not about to surrender their weapons, and a skirmish ensued that cost both sides several casualties.

Three weeks later, another of Chivington's subordinates, Major Jacob Downing, came upon a band of Cheyennes camped near Cedar Bluffs, 60 miles above the South Platte. Although he only suspected them of stealing cattle and horses, Downing launched an attack that killed an estimated 25 Cheyennes and destroyed their lodges and belongings. His report played to Chivington's hard line: "I believe now it is but the commencement of war with this tribe, which must result in exterminating them." In fact, the Cheyenne had shown little appetite for confrontation, but Chivington's forces were doing all they could to incite them.

A further provocation occurred a few days later in western Kansas near the Smoky Hill River, where hundreds of Southern Cheyennes—including parties led by Black Kettle and Lean Bear, another prominent chief who had pledged to keep peace with the whites—were gathered with bands of Sioux to hunt for sorely needed buffalo meat. On May 16, the Cheyennes encountered a column of 54 men of the 1st Colorado under Lieutenant George Eayre. Lean Bear boldly rode forward with another Indian to parley with the bluecoats. The chief wore on his shirt a peace medal presented to him on a recent trip to Washington and carried in his hand a paper signed by President Abraham Lincoln on that same occasion, attesting to his trustworthiness. (After hearing Lincoln speak, Lean Bear had told him that he "had no pockets in which to hide his words, but would treasure them in his heart, and would faithfully carry them back to his people.") Before Lean Bear could present his credentials, however, he and his companion were shot from their horses. "As they lay on the ground," a Cheyenne witness named Wolf Chief said later, "the soldiers rode forward and shot them again."

The killings sparked furious fighting between Cheyenne warriors and Eayre's contingent, which included gun crews from the Colorado Independent Battery who opened fire with two mountain howitzers. According to Eayre, more than two dozen warriors were killed. Nonetheless, the Cheyennes kept up the attack until Black Kettle prevailed on the warriors

John Evans

Colonel John Chivington

ATTENTION!
INDIAN
FIGHTERS

Having been authorized by the Governor to raise a Company of 100 day

U. S. VOL CAVALRY!

For immediate service against hostile Indians. I call upon all who wish to engage in such service to call at my office and enroll their names immediately.

Pay and Rations the same as other U. S. Volunteer Cavalry.

Parties furnishing their own horses will receive 40c per day, and rations for the same, while in the service.

The Company will also be entitled to all horses and other plunder taken from the Indians.

Office first door East of Recorder's Office.

HAL. SAYR.

Central City, Aug. 13, '64.

to pull back and allow Eayre to withdraw with his wounded. It was a characteristic gesture by the Cheyenne peace chief, who once declared that his hand "had never been raised against a white man, woman, or child."

Now Chivington and Evans had the uprising they wanted. Black Kettle could not restrain the Southern Cheyenne after the killing of Lean Bear, and their quest for vengeance took a fearful toll. No longer were the raids limited to stealing livestock or provisions. Cheyenne warriors struck at stagecoaches, wagon trains, and ranches, killing, looting, and burning. Soon other tribes joined in. At Fort Larned, Kiowas staged a women's dance, and while the soldiers were distracted by the ceremony, the warriors stampeded the post's herd of horses. The Arapaho chief Left Hand, intent on proving his friendship for the whites, approached the fort with an offer to help fight the Kiowas and recover the stock—only to be greeted with howitzer shells. In response, young Arapaho warriors banded together with Kiowas to bolster the Cheyenne raiders. By August of 1864, the Indians had killed dozens of white settlers and travelers and had practically isolated the Colorado Territory from eastern mail and stage service.

All summer the settlement of Denver was gripped by fear that was only intensified by the actions and edicts of Governor Evans. After four Northern Arapahos murdered a young rancher, his wife, and two children 20 miles east of the city, Evans put their mutilated bodies on public display. Two days later, a false report that Indians were approaching the town sparked panic. To keep feelings at a fever pitch, Evans issued a proclamation authorizing citizens "to kill and destroy, as enemies of the country, all such hostile Indians." Meanwhile, he was firing off telegrams to Washington pleading for reinforcements. In one dispatch, he predicted the "largest Indian war this country ever had," and sought permission to raise 10,000 volunteers to fight it. His pleas drew skepticism, but he did receive authority from the War Department in August to recruit 100-day volunteers for the 3rd Colorado Cavalry Regiment, which would be dedicated to fighting Indians. Most of those who came forward were idle men of little discipline. To boost enlistments, Colonel Chivington declared martial law, strengthening the impression that the survival of the community was at stake.

One of the few whites trying to cool tempers during these feverish days was William Bent. Late in the summer, he sent a message to Black Kettle and other Southern Cheyenne chiefs calling their attention to an earlier proclamation by Governor Evans that had directed "friendly Indians" to report to military posts for provisions and for their own protection. With that in mind, Bent's son George helped Black Kettle and his fellow

On August 29, 1864, Black Kettle, a leading chief of the Southern Cheyenne, dictated the letter at right proposing peace between his people and the U.S. Army. The chief was a self-described "friend to the whites."

A wagon-borne delegation of Southern Cheyenne and Arapaho chiefs headed by Black Kettle rides into Denver to negotiate peace in September 1864. Although some whites favored a treaty, the "Rocky Mountain News" reflected the sentiments of others: "We are opposed to anything which looks like a treaty of peace with the Indians. The season is near at hand when they can be chastised, and it should be done with no gentle hand."

chiefs draft a conciliatory letter to Major Edward Wynkoop, the new commander of Fort Lyon. Wynkoop—a lanky peacekeeper whom the Cheyenne would refer to affectionately as Tall Chief—welcomed this opportunity to avert further bloodshed. He led a detachment of 127 mounted men on a journey of nearly 100 miles to the headwaters of the Smoky Hill River, where Black Kettle's Southern Cheyennes were camped with Dog Soldiers, Arapahos, and Sioux. Arriving there in September, Wynkoop encountered more than 500 angry warriors, who appeared eager for his scalp. Black Kettle calmed them down, and with the aid of an interpreter, he and Wynkoop conferred, each man soon winning the other's respect. Black Kettle told his people that Wynkoop had not come "with a forked tongue or with two hearts, but his words are straight and his heart single." Wynkoop later praised the chief for his "innate dignity and lofty bearing, combined with his sagacity and intelligence."

Wynkoop then led a delegation of Southern Cheyenne and Arapaho leaders, headed by Black Kettle, to Camp Weld near Denver to meet with Governor Evans. Black Kettle greeted Evans in council there on September 28 with a passionate appeal. "All we ask is that we may have peace with the whites," the chief said. "We want to hold you by the hand. You are our father; we have been traveling through a cloud; the sky has been dark ever since the war began. We want to take good tidings home to our people, that they may sleep in peace. I want you to give all the chiefs of the soldiers here to understand that we are for peace, and that we have made peace, that we may not be mistaken by them for enemies. I have not come here with a little wolf's bark, but have come to talk plain with you."

Evans answered Black Kettle's earnestness with evasions and recriminations. In truth, the council embarrassed him. He had no intention of stifling the war frenzy he had whipped up. As he put it privately to Wynkoop, volunteers for the 3rd Colorado were being "raised to kill Indians, and they must kill Indians." His sentiments were echoed the day the council convened in a telegram from the U.S. regional military commander at Fort Leavenworth in Kansas, Major General Samuel Curtis. "I want no peace," said Curtis, "till the Indians suffer more."

Yet in closing the council, the blunt-spoken territorial commander, Colonel Chivington, unwittingly offered the Indians a way out. "My rule of fighting white men or Indians is to fight them until they lay down their arms and submit to military authority," he told Black Kettle and others of the delegation. "You are nearer Major Wynkoop than anyone else, and you can go to him when you get ready to do that." The Indians took Chivington at his word and left the council content that peace had been made. During October, some 650 Arapahos arrived at Fort Lyon and remained near the post under Wynkoop's assurance of protection and provisions. About the same time, Black Kettle began moving toward the post with some 600 Cheyennes. Then, early in November, there was an ominous change at Fort Lyon: Wynkoop was relieved for being too friendly with the Indians. Command reverted to Major Anthony, who advised the Cheyennes not to report to Fort Lyon but to remain at their camp on Sand Creek, 40 miles to the northeast. They would be safe there, he assured them.

In fact, the willingness of these Indians to "submit to military authority," as Chivington had demanded, put them very much at risk. Pressure was building in Denver for an offensive. Newspapers ridiculed Chivington for inactivity and mocked his inexperienced regiment as the Bloodless Third. With the regiment's enlistment term due to expire in less than a month, Chivington needed a ready target. Rather than chase after bands that had refused to submit, he set his sights on Black Kettle and his people, whose very compliance made them easy marks. Assembling units from the new 3rd Colorado and the old 1st, he led them through deep snow to Fort Lyon, arriving there on November 28.

Major Anthony welcomed Chivington cordially and invited him to fill out his battalions with troops from the post's garrison. The offer infuriated several of Anthony's subordinates at Fort Lyon, who had served under Wynkoop and felt bound by promises of protection he had made to Black Kettle. Lieutenant Joseph Cramer, for one, protested that the planned attack amounted to murder. "Wynkoop had pledged his word as an officer and a man to those Indians," he told Chivington, and "all officers under him were indirectly pledged in the same manner." Chivington responded with raw fury: "Damn any man who is in sympathy with an Indian!"

Chivington left the fort that evening with 700 mounted men and a battery of four 12-pound mountain howitzers. Several officers under him embarked with heavy hearts. Lieutenant Cramer was assigned to command Company K of the 1st Colorado, while Lieutenant Silas Soule, who was equally opposed to the attack, took charge of Company D. The most reluctant participant was William Bent's eldest son, Robert, who was forced at gunpoint to guide the columns through the night to the encampment on Sand Creek, which sheltered some 50 Arapahos and 600 Cheyennes. Among them were young Bent's two brothers and one of his sisters.

The village was cradled in a sharp bend of Sand Creek, where the dry streambed, running south, veered eastward. At dawn on November 29, a

Indians and soldiers gather for a portrait following the September 1864 peace conference at Camp Weld near Denver. Although no treaty was signed at the meeting, Black Kettle (seated, third from left) and his fellow chiefs believed that their people would be allowed to live unmolested near Fort Lyon under the watchful eye of its commander, Major Edward Wynkoop (kneeling, left).

Cheyenne woman out foraging heard the pounding of hoofs in the distance and cried out that buffalo were coming. But soon the villagers could see a host of bluecoats deploying on a ridge along the south bank as other soldiers crossed to the north side to stampede the horses grazing east of the camp. Alerted to the threat in his lodge, Black Kettle hastily took out an American flag that had been given him by the U.S. commissioner of Indian affairs and displayed it alongside a white flag at the end of a lodgepole. Then he stood in front of his tipi, waving his arms and urging his people to remain calm. They had been promised the protection of the troops, he reminded them. There was nothing to fear.

With Black Kettle at the time was White Antelope, another old war leader who had ventured down the path of peace. Now about 70 years of age, White Antelope decided to appeal directly to the soldiers and walked toward them with his hands held high, imploring them in clear English not to shoot. When they dismounted and raised their rifles, he halted in the middle of the streambed, folded his arms over his chest in a gesture of submission, and offered up his death song. "Nothing lives long," he chanted, "except the earth and the mountains." A volley slammed into him, and he slumped forward dead.

The sudden attack threw the villagers into panic. A few men grabbed their weapons and tried to form a line of defense near the creek, but a flurry of canister from the howitzers scattered them. A larger group of about 100 warriors, women, and children fled upstream and sought refuge in hollows they frantically scooped out of the sand. Soldiers surrounded them, pouring in a withering fire, but the warriors resisted to the end. "I never saw more bravery displayed by any set of people on the face of the earth than by these Indians," conceded Major Anthony. "They would charge on the whole company singly, determined to kill someone before being killed themselves."

At least one officer, Lieutenant Soule, held back from the massacre. He kept his men on the south bank and refused to issue them orders to fire. Other officers lost control of their men as the assault degenerated into a murderous free-for-all. Army interpreter John Smith noted that most of the troops "were scattered in different directions, running after small parties of Indians who were trying to escape."

Black Kettle remained in front of his lodge until nearly all the women and children had fled. Then, as he and his wife, Medicine Woman Later, started up the creek, a bullet knocked her to the sand bar. Black Kettle knelt to examine her and then left her for dead. Eight more shots were fired into her. When Black Kettle returned under cover of darkness to retrieve her body, he discovered to his astonishment that she was still alive.

Few others who were cut down were so fortunate, for Chivington had made it clear he wanted no prisoners. "Kill and scalp all, big and little," he had proclaimed. "Nits make lice." John Smith testified to the consequences for those caught in the attack: "They were scalped, their brains knocked out; the men used their knives, ripped open women, clubbed little children, knocked them in the head with their guns, beat their brains out, mutilated their bodies in every sense of the word." Among the trophies taken by the soldiers were the private parts of men and women.

"All did nobly," Chivington boasted of the rampaging soldiers in his official report. The colonel claimed he had lost just nine dead and 38 wounded and had killed more than 400 Indians. The actual Indian toll was less than half that, but appalling nonetheless. When Major Wynkoop learned of

In a painting based on battle reports, cavalrymen attack Black Kettle's village at Sand Creek, Colorado, on November 29, 1864. Ignoring the American and white flags the Cheyennes raised to signal friendship (center), the troops went on a rampage, crushing the resistance hastily mounted by Black Kettle's men and gunning down fleeing women and children. "From the suckling babe to the old warrior, all who were overtaken were deliberately murdered," concluded one government investigative committee.

the attack, he was wild with rage, and the scathing report he later filed on the incident helped bring the bloodbath to light. Two congressional committees investigated the assault and blasted Chivington for what became known as the Sand Creek Massacre.

The official denunciations were small solace for Black Kettle, who lost face as angry warriors from his band joined with the Dog Soldiers and their militant allies among the Sioux and Arapaho. Far from making the region safe for whites, Chivington's actions exposed them to fresh attacks in what was usually the quietest time of year. In the depths of winter, large war parties destroyed depots and ranches, killed or captured their occupants, and made off with 1,500 head of cattle. The most spectacular act of

at the Sand Creek Massacre

retribution occurred in January 1865 at the town of Julesburg, Colorado, along the South Platte, where 1,000 warriors sacked the stage station and cut down telegraph poles to provide fuel for a huge victory dance, held within sight of the soldiers and civilians huddled in nearby Fort Rankin. When the warriors could not lure the soldiers out to fight, they returned to Julesburg and destroyed the remainder of the settlement.

For William Bent, Chivington's assault and the ensuing reprisals marked the fulfillment of his worst fears. None of his children died at Sand Creek, but the massacre tore his family apart. In the aftermath, his son Charles rode with the avenging Dog Soldiers and feuded with brother George when the latter renounced such raids. At one point, Charles threatened to kill both George and his father for consorting with the likes of those who had murdered their Cheyenne kin at Sand Creek. Battle lines were drawn at the deepest level—in the hearts and minds of men of mixed blood, who felt compelled to defend one side of their heritage and defy the

In his drawing of the Sand Creek battle, warrior Howling Wolf depicts himself and three comrades fleeing fierce gunfire while before them are more soldiers, rifles blazing.

The dagger shown here was found on the battlefield at the Sand Creek Massacre. Its Cheyenne owner crafted his own bone hilt for a manufactured blade. He fashioned a sheath for the weapon by fastening the folded leather with soft lead rivets.

other. And the struggle had scarcely begun.

Even as Chivington was marshaling forces for the slaughter at Sand Creek, a separate conflict was brewing to the south, this one pitting federal troops against Comanches, Kiowas, and Kiowa Apaches. The objective of those U.S. forces was not to halt the intensifying forays by the allied tribes against the Texans, who had sided with the Confederacy and were thus considered worthy of such punishment. Instead, the Federals hoped to put an end to Indian attacks on traffic along the Santa Fe Trail, their lifeline to loyal New Mexico.

For the warriors involved, such raids were an honorable pastime—an indispensable way for men to prove their worth and sustain their families now that whites had significantly restricted their domain and disrupted their hunting grounds. Comanche territory had once embraced much of western Texas, for example, but determined onslaughts by Texas Rangers and other Indian fighters had pushed the tribe up into the rugged Panhandle and environs. Some bands of Comanches had even accepted confinement to reservations, but most continued to roam with allied Kiowas, preying on buffalo when possible and supplementing that dwindling resource with whatever they could glean through plunder.

In November 1864, General James Carleton, commander of federal forces in New Mexico, dispatched the noted frontiersman Christopher (Kit) Carson at the head of the 1st New Mexico Cavalry Regiment to punish the Kiowas and Comanches for recent assaults on the Santa Fe Trail. Carson, accompanied by some 300 cavalrymen and 100 Ute and Jicarilla Apache auxiliaries—who were fighting to support their families—left Fort Bascom in New Mexico and headed east into Texas along the Canadian River, seeking out the winter camps of the targeted tribes. After two weeks on the trail, the soldiers came upon a large Kiowa village containing 170 lodges and as many as 1,000 inhabitants. Carson's force struck the village at dawn on November 25, just four days before the Sand Creek Massacre. Unlike Black Kettle's Cheyennes, the Kiowas had no reason to expect mercy from the bluecoats and were prepared for the worst. Warriors mounted horses that were tethered close to their lodges in case of attack and challenged Carson's troopers, enabling other fighting men to retreat safely downstream with the women and children to a place called Adobe Walls— the remains of an old trading post once operated by the Bent family.

In the midst of the attack, the leader of the Kiowa band, an old chief named Dohausen, hurried off to seek help from a neighboring Comanche village, completing the journey on foot after his horse was shot out from under him. By the time the bluecoats reached Adobe Walls, more than 1,000 armed Kiowas and Comanches were waiting for them. Carson ordered his men to dismount and spread out in a wide skirmish line. Thus dispersed, they faced repeated charges by the expert Indian horsemen, who knew how to use their mounts as screens against enemy fire. As Lieutenant George Pettis of Carson's artillery reported, the Comanches and Kiowas attacked obliquely, "with their bodies thrown over the sides of their horses, at a full run, and shooting occasionally under their horses' necks." The Kiowa warrior Stumbling Bear mounted so many charges that his daughter's shawl, which he wore for luck, was pierced by a dozen bullets, but he emerged unscathed.

The determined warriors used every stratagem at their disposal to confound their foes. One man equipped with a bugle confused Carson's troops by blowing bogus command signals, while others set fire to the grass and came at the bluecoats through clouds of smoke. Only well-placed shots from two mountain howitzers commanded by Lieutenant Pettis held the Kiowas and Comanches at bay. Fortunate to extricate his troops, Carson turned around and burned the lodges in the Kiowa village. Then he hurried with his troopers back to New Mexico. He claimed 60 Indian dead, against three of his own. "I flatter myself that I have taught these Indians a severe lesson," he wrote. Yet he conceded that his opponents had shown exceptional daring and doubted that one such assault would be enough to end the strife.

Neither Carson's foray nor Chivington's massacre inspired much hope in Washington that punitive expeditions alone would soon bring tranquillity to the region. In the years to come, federal policy toward the tribes of the Southern Plains would veer back and forth between accommodation and coercion, as officials strained to end the turmoil one way or the other be-

The slaughter at Sand Creek sparked Indian raids on stagecoaches, like the one portrayed below, as well as attacks on ranches and towns all across the Southern Plains. Declared one Cheyenne leader: "The white man has taken our country, killed all our game; was not satisfied with that, but killed our wives and children. Now no peace. We have raised the battle-ax until death."

fore it stalled the momentum of westward expansion. With the end of the Civil War in April 1865, a fresh wave of migration broke over the Plains, stirred up by legislation such as the Homestead Act, which granted land to white settlers, and congressional charters that licensed the construction of railroads across the West. Anxious to clear Indians from the path of progress, authorities offered tribes both the olive branch and the sword.

The first move went to the peacemakers. Beginning in August of 1865, chiefs of the Comanche, Kiowa, and Kiowa Apache gathered with leaders of the Southern Cheyenne and Arapaho near the mouth of the Little Arkansas River in southern Kansas to confer with a skilled group of government negotiators, including William Bent and Kit Carson—who was respected for his honesty even by his former Indian foes. Among the chiefs attending the council were men who had faced attack by white troops, including Black Kettle and Dohausen. Black Kettle came reluctantly, bringing with him only a small portion of his scattered tribe and grieving at having exposed his people to attack at Sand Creek. "My shame is as big as the earth," he confessed. His wife accompanied him, and witnesses examined the nine wounds she had suffered. The text of the treaty agreed upon at the council provided Black Kettle with some vindication by repudiating the "gross and wanton outrage" perpetrated at Sand Creek and offering Indians whose kin had died in the massacre restitution in the form of extra allotments of land.

Kiowa warrior Stumbling Bear, shown wearing an army coat with the insignia of a major general—probably given to him by Winfield Scott Hancock—fought courageously at Adobe Walls in Texas against a cavalry assault led by Colonel Kit Carson on November 25, 1864. Acknowledging the ferocity of his foes, Carson wrote in his official report, "I must say they acted with more daring and bravery than I have ever before seen."

While attempting to redress old wrongs, however, the pacts agreed to by Black Kettle and the chiefs of other tribes failed to avert further strife because neither the whites nor the Indians were able to secure the compliance of outside parties whose cooperation was essential. In exchange for a pledge by the Comanche and Kiowa to refrain from "violence and injury to the frontier settlements and to travelers on the Santa Fe road," those tribes were supposed to retain as a reservation much of their existing homeland, including the entire Texas Panhandle. But the agreement required approval from the state of Texas, and legislators there refused to go along, negating the deal. The Southern Cheyenne and Arapaho, for their part, were allotted a sizable new reservation extending southward from the Arkansas River in central Kansas. But Kansas, like Texas, balked at accepting a large reservation within its boundaries. In any case, the Dog

Soldiers and other defiant Cheyenne and Arapaho bands who were absent from the council neither knew nor cared about the terms of the treaty. They continued to frequent their old hunting grounds above the Arkansas River and prey on traffic along the Smoky Hill Trail to Denver.

This threat to the emigration corridor drew a stern response from the army commander of the Department of the Missouri, Major General Winfield Scott Hancock. Renowned for his role in turning back the Confederates at Gettysburg in 1863, Hancock knew little about Indians and found it hard to assess the often-contradictory reports he received on their activities. By the spring of 1867, he was besieged with rumors of an impending Indian uprising, some of them instigated by the railroads to ensure protection for their construction crews. Hancock decided to act. In early April, he assembled at Fort Larned an army of 1,400 men so exhaustively equipped that they even had pontoons for bridging the region's normally shallow streams in case of spring floods. "We go prepared for war and will make it if a proper occasion presents," he proclaimed. "No insolence will be tolerated." Then he marched westward to pacify any hostile Indians in the area.

In this unidentified battle scene, which was drawn by a Kiowa warrior, soldiers dug into a defensive position fire desperately at Kiowa fighters encircling them. At Adobe Walls and other battles, the federal troops sometimes found themselves besieged by swarms of expert Indian horsemen.

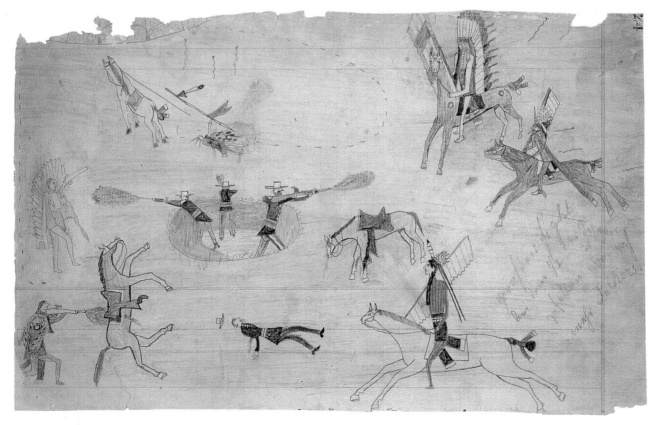

Hancock's advance evoked bitter memories for the man serving as Indian agent for the Cheyennes in the general's path—Edward Wynkoop, the former army major who had earlier witnessed the consequences of Chivington's punitive campaign. Now as then, Wynkoop believed, rumors of an Indian uprising were being used to justify a show of force that was more likely to incite native hostility than repress it. Hancock's march put him on a collision course with a large band of Cheyennes—mostly Dog Soldiers—who were camped with some Sioux on Pawnee Fork, 40 miles west of Fort Larned. Wynkoop pleaded with Hancock to steer clear of the village. When Hancock insisted on confronting the Indians camped there, Wynkoop rode with him in the hope of serving as mediator.

On April 13, the marching bluecoats were confronted a few miles east of the Indian village by several hundred Cheyenne and Sioux warriors, armed to the teeth and poised to contest Hancock's advance. To Hancock's subordinate, 27-year-old Lieutenant Colonel George Armstrong Custer—the flaxen-haired boy wonder of Civil War fame—the warriors presented "one of the finest and most imposing military displays, prepared according to the Indian art of war, which it has ever been my lot to behold."

Wynkoop, intent on avoiding a showdown, rode forward alone to seek a parley, and returned shortly with a delegation of chiefs led by a Cheyenne named Roman Nose—so called by whites for that distinctive facial feature. Roman Nose was an awesome figure who stood six feet three inches tall, with a broad chest

At a deserted encampment at Pawnee Fork, Kansas, an elderly Sioux sits forlornly in his tipi. The Cheyennes and Sioux abandoned the village in April 1867 on learning of the impending arrival of a punitive expedition led by Major General Winfield Scott Hancock. Compelled to travel quickly, the fleeing Indians left the old man, whose leg was broken, to be taken prisoner by Hancock.

Having helped themselves to buffalo robes, beaded moccasins, and other plunder, federal troops burn the Indian village at Pawnee Fork in April 1867. The conflagration was intended to punish the Cheyenne and Sioux warriors for their raids along a vital stagecoach route. Instead, it provoked a series of retaliatory attacks by the Indians.

and taut muscles that lay coiled "under the bronze of his skin," said an army officer, "like twisted wire." He met Hancock with four revolvers in his belt, a bow in his hand, and a carbine dangling at the side of his pony.

The ensuing conference was tense. Roman Nose was inclined to kill Hancock on the spot, but a companion dissuaded him on the grounds that their women and children would suffer for it. Instead, the chief prolonged the parley for some time, then withdrew with the assembled warriors to their village, followed closely by the bluecoats, who discovered when they got there that the women and children had profited by the delay and fled. That night, the chiefs and warriors slipped away to join them, and an exasperated Hancock sent Custer in pursuit. When Custer reported a few days later that fresh depredations had been committed along the Smoky Hill Trail, Hancock chose to blame the fugitives and ordered the burning of the village's 252 lodges and all the food and equipment left behind there.

Hancock's deed helped provoke the very response his campaign was supposed to prevent—fierce attacks by Indians on the vital lines of communication across Kansas. In the Smoky Hill River valley, the raiders stopped stagecoach service and blunted the progress of the Kansas Pacific Railroad by harrying construction crews and prying up rails to wreck an entire train. Alarmed by the toll of Hancock's War, as it came to be known, Washington again shifted gears and pursued a diplomatic settlement.

The resulting peace council, which drew nearly 5,000 Indians to Medicine Lodge Creek, south of Fort Larned, in October 1867, was the last such gathering on the Southern Plains. New reservations were again designated for the tribes of the region, but this time the federal government did not need state approval. Land had recently become available in the Indian Territory—present-day Oklahoma—when the Five Civilized Tribes that had

In a painting by an eyewitness, Indian delegates meet with federal officials in 1867 along Medicine Lodge

Creek in Kansas and reluctantly agree to settle their people on reservations in exchange for annuities.

been relocated there from the southeastern woodlands earlier in the century were compelled to forfeit about half their holdings as punishment for siding with the Confederacy during the Civil War. Some 5,550 square miles of the forfeited land were now set aside for the Comanche, Kiowa, and Kiowa Apache; to the north of that reservation, a somewhat larger area was allotted to the Southern Cheyenne and Arapaho. The goal was not simply to confine the Indians but to coax them down the "white man's road" by persuading them to live in houses and raise crops. Comanche and Kiowa delegates were reluctant to forsake their familiar tipis. "Why do you insist on those houses?" queried the Kiowa chief Satanta. Nonetheless, the longing for annuities and for peace with the remorseless bluecoats induced them to sign.

For Black Kettle, the proposed settlement represented an opportunity to reunite his people after the divisive battle at Sand Creek. Unlike earlier peace councils, this one was attended by the Dog Soldiers and other militant members of the tribe. They were slow to ratify the treaty, however, for they first had to take part in an important communal ritual—the annual renewal of their sacred medicine arrows, thought to confer supernatural power on warriors and hunters. That ceremony may have helped to bring the Southern Cheyennes together, for when they finally appeared at the council site, as many as 500 warriors galloped across the shallow creek in a rousing display of tribal unity, waving lances and firing pistols into the air. Soldiers overseeing the council feared trouble, but the Cheyennes leaped from their horses and began shaking hands all around.

Black Kettle and his fellow chiefs signed the treaty only after receiving verbal assurances that, contrary to language in the document restricting their hunting range to south of the Arkansas, they could still hunt north of that river if they avoided white settlements and roads. Among those who put his mark to the treaty was the longtime Dog Soldier chief, Bull Bear, whose brother Lean Bear had been shot down by white troops three years earlier. Bull Bear pressed the pen so hard that the nib broke through the paper. "I have done it," he said with a grim smile, "and my word shall last."

Government negotiators hoped that the tribes covered by the Medicine Lodge treaty would soon become conditioned to life on the reservation and remain there year-round. But the chiefs who signed saw no reason to dissuade their followers from venturing abroad to hunt buffalo or pursue tribal enemies. Even as officials prepared the reservations for occupancy, war parties and hunting bands continued to stray into areas where run-

Wearing a bonnet endowed with protective powers, Cheyenne chief Roman Nose leads a triumphant war party back to camp in this sketch by one of his warriors, Howling Wolf. The men jubilantly fire their rifles and wave fresh scalps. Even after the signing of the Medicine Lodge treaty, the Indians and whites continued to battle each other on the Plains—and Roman Nose was counted among the casualties.

ins with whites were all but inevitable. One such collision occurred in August 1868, when 200 Southern Cheyenne warriors, joined by some Arapahos and Sioux, went on a rampage in Kansas. Reportedly, the warriors were returning from an ill-fated raid against rival Pawnees when one of them approached a homesteader to ask for food and was rebuffed with a shotgun blast. The incident inflamed the warriors, who were fortified with whiskey and smarting from their recent setback. Lashing out at the whites in their path, they looted, burned, and raped, claiming a dozen lives.

This alarming spree, and lesser instances of violence, weakened the hold of the peacemakers on the frontier. Edward Wynkoop argued in vain for a policy that would identify and punish specific wrongdoers without alienating entire bands. Disillusioned, he resigned as Indian agent, and

Black Kettle's people lost their strongest defender among the whites.

As fall approached, the army stepped up its efforts to track down Indian bands that were roaming above the Arkansas River within reach of white homesteaders, travelers, or construction crews. Among the units dispatched was a special scouting outfit, commanded by Colonel George Forsyth and composed of 50 seasoned frontiersmen. On September 17, 1868, Forsyth's scouts were camped on the Arikaree branch of the Republican River, in northeastern Colorado, where they hoped to surprise and subdue a mixed band of Cheyennes and Sioux they had been tracking for some time. Suddenly, about dawn, they found themselves besieged by Indians who "seemed to spring from the very earth," as one report put it. Forsyth's scouts took refuge on a small, brush-covered sand bar in the shallow river, and fired back with their Spencer repeating carbines and Colt revolvers. The Indians—several hundred warriors in all—came at them in waves, sweeping by on either side of the island, their bodies slung low on their horses for protection.

Chief Roman Nose was one of the leaders of the band, but he was missing from these initial charges because, according to Cheyenne lore, he had broken a taboo. Tradition dictated that the owner of the special war bonnet he wore in battle must never eat food served with an iron instrument. Roman Nose recently had eaten bread served him by a Sioux woman with an iron fork. He feared that until there was time to undergo the necessary purification rites, his war bonnet's protective medicine would be fatally compromised. About noon, however, after the first attacks had been rebuffed by Forsyth's scouts, Roman Nose reluctantly agreed to lead the next charge. He stripped to leggings, breechcloth, and moccasins; striped his face with war paint; strapped on cartridge belt, quiver, and bow; and donned his famous war bonnet—a magnificent beaded buckskin headdress studded with a single polished buffalo horn and eagle feathers that trailed down his back and alongside his pony.

The sight of the chief preparing for battle filled the discouraged warriors with new hope. An old Sioux medicine man beat his drum and shouted exhortations. Indian women and children danced and sang. Then Roman Nose threw back his head and let out a piercing war whoop. With his followers close behind, he galloped downstream, buffalo-skin shield in one hand, rifle and reins in the other. Roman Nose led assault after assault into the teeth of enemy fire. Finally, as he raced by the scouts and reached the far end of the island, a bullet caught him in the back. He managed somehow to ride back to camp, where he died the next morning.

Taken prisoner by the army, three Southern Cheyenne leaders—(from left to right) Curly Hair, Fat Bear, and Lean Face—rest en route to Fort Hays, Kansas, where they would be held as hostages to ensure that their followers moved to the reservation. Curly Hair and Lean Face were among the delegates who signed the Medicine Lodge treaty in 1867. Both were killed in May 1869 in a scuffle with guards at Fort Hays; Fat Bear was clubbed during the incident but survived.

Sobered by the loss of Roman Nose and by the wall of fire from the well-armed defenders, the Indians settled down for a siege. On the ninth day, the 10th U.S. Cavalry, a regiment alerted by two of Forsyth's messengers, arrived to relieve the beleaguered scouts. By then most of the warriors had slipped away with their families.

The punishment absorbed by Forsyth's scouts only stiffened the resolve of the indefatigable general who was now overseeing the army's efforts in the West, William Tecumseh Sherman. His objective was to drive the southern tribes in their entirety onto the new reservations specified by treaty—or else. "All who cling to their old hunting grounds are hostile and will remain so till killed off," he announced. To enforce this policy, he directed the new commander of the Department of the Missouri, Major General Philip Sheridan, to employ the tactics of total war that Sherman had used so effectively against the Confederates during the Civil War. Instead of seeking out elusive war parties on the open prairie, the army would strike at the bands that harbored them. To that end, the bluecoats would resort to the proven method of attacking Indian villages in the winter, when the occupants were least mobile and most vulnerable. By destroying food, shelter, and horses, and rounding up the families of fighting men, they would break the warriors' will and deprive them of support. No peace would be made with a tribe until it admitted defeat.

Sheridan's plans called for three columns to proceed from army posts

in New Mexico, Colorado, and Kansas and converge on the Indian Territory. Peaceful bands seeking sanctuary there would be spared; all others would be subject to attack. The designated reservations were not yet ready to receive the tribes, so Sherman proposed that Fort Cobb on the Washita River serve as a temporary refuge for friendly Indians—a group he characterized as the "old, young, and feeble," since he assumed that the able-bodied men were inherently hostile.

By late November, more than 6,000 men, women, and children from the affected tribes had camped along the Washita River near Fort Cobb, where they hoped to avoid retribution. Their presence posed a problem for the fort's commander, General William Hazen. Sherman had informed him that Sheridan's oncoming troops might pursue hostile Indians near Fort

On November 27, 1868, Custer and his 7th Cavalry charge through a Cheyenne village situated on the Washita River near Fort Cobb. Among the warriors killed that day was Black Kettle, who had led his people to the Washita in the hope of finding sanctuary.

Cobb, and Hazen concluded that he should offer sanctuary only to those bands that were friendly. Whatever their intentions may have been, Sherman and his men had created a trap for Indians around the fort. Those denied refuge there would be easy prey for the converging columns.

Among the chiefs seeking sanctuary was Black Kettle. Still hoping for peace, he told Hazen that he wanted to move his people to Fort Cobb. Although Hazen had already welcomed some Kiowas and Comanches, he rebuffed Black Kettle, explaining that Sheridan considered Black Kettle's Cheyennes hostile. "We want peace," Black Kettle insisted, while admitting that he had limited control over his warriors. "Some will not listen," he said, "and since the fighting began, I have not been able to keep them all at home." Hazen told Black Kettle that he would have to make peace with Sheridan—a hopeless task, since Sheridan's men were already on the way and were prepared to attack any band not under Hazen's protection.

No one was more eager to strike the first blow than Lieutenant Colonel Custer, whose 7th U.S. Cavalry Regiment was at the forefront of the column moving south from Kansas under Sheridan's leadership. Custer had accomplished little in Hancock's War and had much to prove as an Indian fighter. Departing Kansas on November 23 with Osage Indian scouts, his men picked up tracks in the snow and followed the trail of the presumed hostiles directly to Black Kettle's camp on the Washita.

On November 27, Black Kettle awoke to the blare of a military band playing "Garry Owen," an old Irish drinking tune Custer had adopted as the 7th Cavalry's march. Then came the blast of Colts and carbines as the cavalrymen stormed the village. Young warriors burst from their lodges and put up a furious resistance so that others might escape. This time, Black Kettle made no effort to restore calm or discourage flight. Joining in the exodus, he and his wife mounted a pony he kept tethered next to his lodge. They were partway across the shallow Washita when bullets slammed into them from behind and knocked them facedown into the icy water.

Custer proudly cited Black Kettle among the 103 Cheyenne men he reported killed in the attack, but he was reticent about the slaying of Medicine Woman Later and other noncombatants. In fact, the true Cheyenne death toll was closer to 60, roughly two-thirds of whom were women and children. Custer's force may actually have killed fewer men at Washita than it lost, for 22 of his soldiers died—17 of them in a detachment that pursued some fleeing villagers downstream, only to be intercepted and annihilated by warriors roused from nearby camps, of whose existence the reckless Custer had been unaware.

Shown wearing a presidential peace medal, Kiowa leader Satanta was a determined warrior who led his men on bold raids into Texas and Mexico long after other Plains tribes had submitted to federal authority. The shield he carried was a family heirloom made in 1795 that had protected his father and grandfather.

Sheridan and Sherman later defended the attack and credited the punitive campaign with forcing thousands of Indians to honor the Treaty of Medicine Lodge. By the spring of 1869, most southern tribe members were settling on their reservations. But the land was stained with blood and haunted by betrayal, and little but resentment would grow there.

Black Kettle's fate cast a long shadow over other chiefs who had to accept the limits of reservation life or risk punishment of the sort meted out at Washita. Among those who chose the path of defiance was the Kiowa leader Satanta, who had assumed a leading role among his people following the death of Dohausen in 1866. Dohausen had been committed to peace, but his passing left a void, enabling warriors such as Satanta to rise to the fore. White officials scarcely knew what to make of this mercurial figure, who could be ingratiating one moment and insolent the next. He loved to talk and gloried in pomp; painted his lodge bright red and spread the floor with carpets for guests; and announced meals by blowing on a French horn. General Hancock had once tried to placate Satanta by presenting him with a major general's dress uniform, complete with plumed hat. Resplendent in his new garb, the chief had repaid Hancock by running off the mule herd at Fort Dodge—and doffing his plumed hat in a parting salute.

For Satanta as for many other Kiowas and Comanches, the Treaty of Medicine Lodge was a pact with the bluecoats—not with the tribes' old adversaries, the white settlers of Texas. The raids into Texas had persisted, and they continued after the Indians moved to the reservation. The raiders were egged on by the Quahada, a band of nearly 2,000 Comanches who had never signed a treaty and still roamed the plateau called the Staked Plain in the Texas Panhandle and eastern New Mexico. Reservation Comanches and Kiowas would venture across the Red River into Texas, where they often joined up with Quahadas before embarking on a raid. Afterward, they would ride back to Fort Sill, their new agency on the reservation, to rejoin their families and receive annuities—safe in the knowledge that no pursuing Texans were permitted to enter the reservation.

In May 1871, Satanta led some 100 Kiowa warriors on such a foray. About 60 miles below the Red River, they set up an ambush on the road to Fort Richardson. A lone coach escorted by 15 cavalrymen came in view, and the Indians prepared to attack. But their medicine man, Mamanti, advised against it. Based on his interpretation of an owl's cry the night before, he predicted that a richer prize would soon appear. The coach the Kiowas let go carried none other than William Tecumseh Sherman, now commanding general of the U.S. Army and on hand to assess complaints from Texans about Indian raids. As prophesied, a more tempting target arrived shortly—10 wagons laden with shelled corn. The Kiowas killed seven of the teamsters manning the wagons and made off with the booty. One of the surviving drivers staggered into Fort Richardson that night and reported the attack to Sherman, who had unknowingly eluded it.

Nine days later, Satanta arrived back at the Fort Sill Agency, where he boasted of his role in the recent raid and sought arms and ammunition, which he planned to use for fresh assaults. Sherman, who had hurried to Fort Sill, confronted Satanta on the front porch of the post commander's quarters and ordered the arrest of the chief and two of his confederates, Satank and Big Tree. In rapid succession, Satanta threw back his blanket and drew a revolver, Sherman shouted a command, and shutters on the front windows flew open to reveal cavalrymen inside, with carbines cocked. Undeterred, a Kiowa warrior pointed his rifle at the general, only to be jumped by the post commander, Colonel Benjamin Grierson.

After things settled down, Satanta, Satank, and Big Tree were manacled and bundled off by wagon train to face trial in Texas. Satank was an elderly chief who was both feared and respected within the tribe for his spirit power. Soon after leaving Fort Sill, he drew a blanket over his head and began chanting the death song of the Koitsenok warrior society, which he headed. Under the blanket, he worked his hands free of their shackles, and then attacked his guard with a knife he had concealed. (Kiowas would later say Satank had secreted the knife in his gullet and then disgorged it.) Guards in the wagon behind Satank stood up and fired two volleys into him. Thus the old man died, as he had intended, preferring a suicidal escape attempt to imprisonment by white men.

Satanta and Big Tree were found guilty of murder and sentenced to death. Under political pressure from Washington, however, the governor of Texas first commuted the sentences and then pardoned the pair in 1873, prompting an outraged protest from Sherman. "I believe Satanta and Big Tree will have their revenge," he wrote to the governor, "and that if they are to have scalps, that yours is the first that should be taken."

The unrest on the reservation went far beyond the trouble stirred up by a few war chiefs, however. Neither farming nor government rations provided the Indians with the sustenance and satisfaction they had long derived from buffalo hunting. Many bands continued to venture out in

In a sketch by Kiowa artist Zotom, army officers accept the surrender of a band of Kiowas camped in the Wichita Mountains of southern Indian Territory. One such group, led by warrior Big Bow, raided settlements in Texas and the Indian Territory for at least a decade before surrendering in 1875.

search of prey, but the buffalo were vanishing. Beginning about 1870, white hunters armed with high-powered rifles ranged southward from central Kansas into the Texas Panhandle, where the Indians retained exclusive hunting rights under the Medicine Lodge treaty. In just three years, from 1872 through 1874, whites killed more than three million buffalo on the Southern Plains. Federal officials for the most part approved the slaughter, for they recognized that the hide hunters were, as General Sheridan put it baldly, "destroying the Indians' commissary."

In response, Southern Cheyennes joined with Comanches and Kiowas in lashing out at the white riflemen. The contest for hunting rights climaxed in June 1874 at a new trading post in the Texas Panhandle frequented by white buffalo hunters. There, within sight of the adobe ruins where Kit Carson had battled the Kiowas in 1864, more than 500 war-

In September 1874, soldiers descended the steep walls of Palo Duro Canyon and attacked Kiowas and Comanches encamped on the canyon floor. Although the Indians escaped, the destruction of their lodges, winter provisions, and pony herds forced them to choose reservation life over starvation.

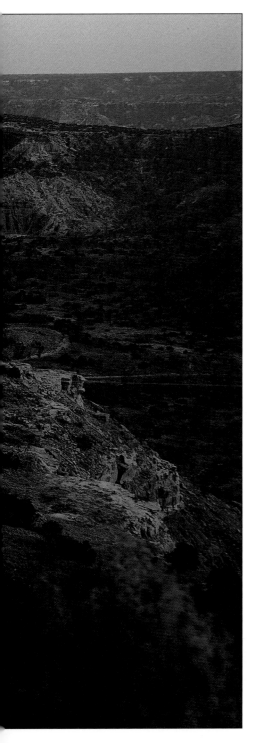

riors—mostly Cheyennes and Comanches, led by a determined Quahada chief named Quanah Parker—stormed the post. In the end, the attackers fell prey to the same lethal weapons that were wiping out the buffalo. Before the Indians withdrew, no fewer than 70 had been killed or wounded by the defenders, who had lost only three men of their own.

This second battle at Adobe Walls set in motion the last great act of defiance by Indians on the Southern Plains. Fearing retaliation and despairing of life on the reservation, the bulk of the Cheyennes, Comanches, and Kiowas—nearly 5,000 people in all—fled westward and took refuge in the Red River country, leaving only the Arapahos behind in significant numbers. Half-hidden in terrain cleft by canyons and arroyos, the migrants seemed less intent on challenging the white man than on escaping his regime and resuming their old ways. But the troops would not leave them alone. In an engagement in late September that set the tone for this Red River War, as whites called it, the 4th U.S. Cavalry Regiment under Colonel Ranald Mackenzie discovered a vast encampment of Comanches and Kiowas in Palo Duro Canyon, southeast of present-day Amarillo. His horsemen dismounted to descend the steep trail to the canyon floor and took the Indians by surprise. While the fugitives fled up the canyon walls, Mackenzie's men burned hundreds of lodges and all the provisions laid by for the winter, then made off with the Indians' herd of 1,424 horses and mules, cutting out the best animals and shooting the rest.

Such tactics brought the fugitives to the brink of starvation. Through the late fall and winter, disheartened bands surrendered and trekked back to the reservation. By the spring of 1875, virtually all the survivors had returned. Efforts to single out Indians for punishment provoked a breakout by a small band of Cheyennes, but they were soon tracked down and annihilated, effectively ending armed resistance.

To prevent a renewal of hostilities, Lieutenant Richard Pratt picked out a group of 72 Indians—noted chiefs and obscure warriors selected almost at random—and shipped them off to a fortress prison in Florida, where he attempted to reform them. Harsher treatment awaited another chief involved in the Red River War: Satanta. After surrendering, he was returned to the penitentiary in Texas and left to languish under conditions he could not endure. "I love to roam the wide prairie," he had said during the Medicine Lodge council in 1867, "and when I do it, I feel free and happy." But to be confined to one place, he added, was to "grow pale and die." In 1878, ailing and embittered, he leaped to his death from an unbarred upper-story window of his Texas prison. ◆

From the parapet of Fort Marion, Indians wrapped in blankets—and linked by chains—behold the Atlantic Ocean for the first time in this drawing by a Kiowa artist by the name of Zotom. The scene depicts the day after the prisoners' arrival, when many of them still expected to be executed.

On the parapet of Ft Marion

WARRIORS IN A PRISON EXILE

In late April 1875, a group of 72 Indians—Kiowa, Cheyenne, Arapaho, Comanche, and Caddo tribesmen identified as participants in the Red River War—were sentenced without trial to exile. Amid the wailing of their women, the shackled and chained warriors and chiefs were loaded into wagons at Fort Sill to begin what they believed was a journey to death. Guarded by troops under Lieutenant Richard Pratt, the prisoners endured 24 days' grueling travel by wagon, rail, and steamboat before reaching their destination: Fort Marion, a decaying Spanish-built fortress in Saint Augustine, Florida, some 1,300 miles from their beloved Plains.

There the captives learned that their sentence was to be not death but another grim fate—indefinite imprisonment. Within weeks of their arrival, however, they realized that Fort Marion was unlike other prisons, for Pratt, who was in charge of the Indian inmates, saw their period of incarceration as an opportunity to educate, not punish, them, so that they might adapt to life in the white man's world. Indeed, under his guidance, Fort Marion was run more like a school than a prison, and its inmates were granted unprecedented privileges and freedoms.

During the three years the Indians were held in Florida, 28 of the younger warriors, encouraged by Pratt, began to draw. These artists' pictures chronicled not only their free days on the Plains but also their lives at Fort Marion, an experience illustrated on the following pages.

Drawings produced by Fort Marion prisoners were made in sketchbooks such as this, most of which were sold for $2 apiece to tourists visiting the site.

OPENING THE SHACKLES

Locked into cramped, dank casemates upon reaching Fort Marion, the Indians pined for their homeland. Many fell ill and several died before Pratt obtained permission to manage his charges in his own way. About two weeks after the prisoners' arrival, Pratt ordered their shackles removed and soon had them building their own barracks on top of the fort's terreplein. The men were outfitted in army uniforms, and their hair was cut short. A few months later, he replaced the army guards with a company of nearly 50 of the youngest prisoners. Drills and inspections defined the daily regimen. And for the remainder of their three-year imprisonment, according to Pratt, the Indians "guarded themselves without a material mishap."

Supervised by Pratt, smartly uniformed prisoners haul a cannon from the parapet. The gun's removal was part of the physical transformation of Fort Marion from a defensive outpost to the benevolent institution that Pratt envisioned.

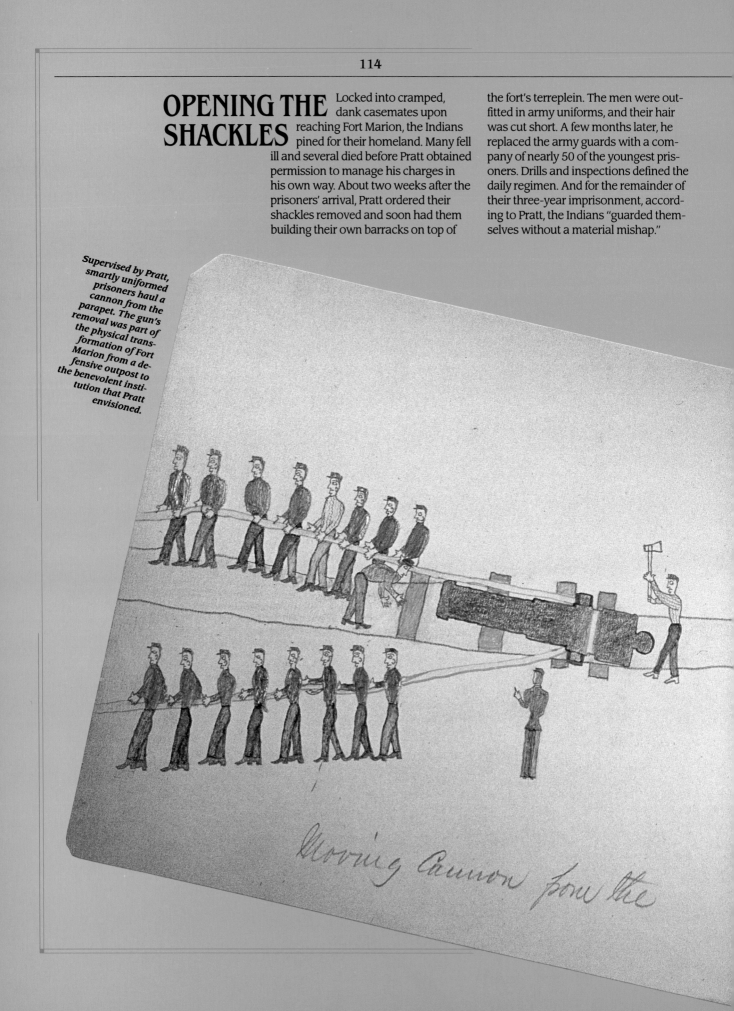

Moving Cannon from the

Indians Shingling their Barracks, Ft Marion

Shackled prisoners face the camera just a few days after their arrival in Saint Augustine, Florida. Many of the detainees suffered from malnutrition that was brought on by months of headlong flight before the relentless pursuit of the U.S. Army troops.

On a beach north of the fort, prisoners snare a strange new prey—a shark, or "water buffalo"—in a tug of war (above). Footraces along the shore were also popular pastimes. The drawing at right shows the men enjoying a campout near the lighthouse on Anastasia Island.

A USEFUL REGIMEN

Believing in the Indians' potential to be educated and to learn a trade, Pratt early on arranged for employment for the prisoners. Local curio dealers paid the men for gathering and polishing sea beans, a tropical seedcase that washed up on the beaches and was a staple souvenir. In addition, the inmates earned money picking and packing oranges, working in a local sawmill, and laboring as firemen and baggage handlers for the local railroad. In time, the men also made money from the drawings and crafts they produced and sold to visitors to the fort.

The earnings from these endeavors provided the Indians not only with funds to send to their families but also with pocket money. Pratt gave them the opportunity to spend the money by issuing passes for unsupervised shopping trips into town.

Another extraordinary freedom the prisoners relished was camping out on the coast. For health and morale, Pratt sent small parties on camping trips "to recuperate by fishing, hunting sea beans, finding material for the canes, bows and arrows which they were permitted to make and sell to visitors."

Drawn by a Cheyenne warrior known as Buffalo Meat, this pictographic price list displays the various goods—ranging from lamps to umbrellas to civilian clothing for off-duty hours—that the prisoners were permitted to purchase in Saint Augustine.

Sightseers at Fort Marion pose for the camera with Indian guards (left). A number of the visitors forged strong friendships with individual prisoners.

Painted with colorful Indian scenes, ladies' fans such as this were crafted by the inmates for sale. In time, the fans became a fad item among the tourists.

MIXING WITH THE WHITES

To "correct the unwarranted prejudice promoted among our people against the Indians" and to "remove from the Indian's mind his false notion that the greedy and vicious among our frontier outlaws fairly represented the white race," Pratt cultivated interaction between the prisoners and white society. During the winter months, thousands of well-heeled northerners flocked to Saint Augustine, a popular resort, and curiosity seekers among them visited the fort, mixing freely with the Indian prisoners and eagerly buying their artwork as souvenirs.

A number of visitors with more serious intent appeared, including Bishop Henry B. Whipple, who ministered to the Indians for a summer; Harriet Beecher Stowe, who wrote of Pratt's experiment in northern journals; and several "excellent ladies" enlisted by Pratt to teach daily English classes for the men.

A picture by a Cheyenne named Cohoe depicts scantily clad prisoners performing a war dance before a paying audience of genteel whites in March 1876. Pratt occasionally granted permission for such events in order to raise money for the institution.

On the reservation in 1897, Zotom paints a model tipi for use in a Smithsonian exhibit. Ordained an Episcopal deacon three years after leaving Fort Marion, Zotom eventually became a medicine man in the Kiowa homeland.

A HARD HOMECOMING

In April 1878, the prisoners were granted freedom after Pratt convinced his superiors that the Indians had been converted to the white man's way. Most returned to the reservation, but 22 of the former warriors, many of whom had adopted Christianity, chose to stay in the East to continue their education. Some of these entered the ministry; others attended Hampton Institute in Virginia—a school for freed black slaves—or later, Carlisle Indian School, which was founded by Pratt in Pennsylvania. Pratt's goal of assimilating the Indians appeared off to an auspicious start.

But that appearance was deceptive. Eventually all of his charges returned to the Indian Territory, where their hopes for sharing their new learning were shattered by the harsh realities of reservation life: poverty, chronic hunger, and disease. As Buffalo Meat wrote to Pratt, "Here we are often hungry and always poor." Disillusioned, most of the former prisoners abandoned the white man's road and his religion.

Perhaps the most notable exception was Making Medicine, a Cheyenne later known as David Pendleton Oakerhater. He served as an Episcopal minister until his death in 1931, and in 1986, he was elevated to sainthood by that church.

Forsaking words for pictures, Etahdleuh, a Kiowa, penned this letter to inform his friend Zotom that he would soon take a train homeward to the reservation. As Pratt's protégé, Etahdleuh spent the better part of 10 years in the East before returning home in 1888, just three months before his death.

ON PATROL FOR THE BLUECOATS

Northern Cheyenne scouts in army dress gather in camp with their commander, Lieutenant Edward Casey (seated on log), who recruited them in the late 1880s in order to keep the peace around their reservation in Montana.

Whites called them scouts, but to their fellow Indians they were known as "wolves": men who prowled the country, searching for signs of the enemy. Some wore wolf skins to elude detection and invoke the animal's cunning spirit; others howled like wolves to warn of danger. As one warrior put it, a scout was like a lone wolf, "looking, looking, looking, all the time."

Such keen observers, with their intimate knowledge of the terrain, were much sought after by army officers pursuing defiant tribes in unfamiliar country. Although some

soldiers feared that these recruits would betray them out of loyalty to their race, the scouts, like their kin, defined themselves not as Indians but as members of distinct tribes or peoples. To most warriors, the pursuit of native rivals—even at the behest of the white man—came as naturally as hunting the buffalo.

Tribal animosities aside, wolves who scouted for the federal troops—and often fought alongside them in battle—sought such rewards as the chance to claim sleek ponies from the enemy and steady pay from the army. "What first took the heart out of my body," an Arikara recruit recalled appreciatively, "was the sight of the green paper money in my hands." Above all, enlisting in the service of the government gave men who were languishing on reservations a sense of purpose. Following the scouts' lead, other tribesmen subsequently affirmed their warrior heritage by serving as reservation police or as troopers in all-Indian cavalry units. As a Crow fighting man remarked of his stint with the army, "It was the only way open for us."

Pawnee scouts wearing traditional garb and government peace medals sit for a portrait with a mixed-blood comrade (center). In the late 1860s, Pawnee recruits helped the army protect construction crews working on the Union Pacific Railroad from raids by hostile Indians.

A Pawnee named White Horse, shown here grasping a ceremonial pipe tomahawk, was among many who served with the army against rival Sioux and Cheyennes.

With his cartridge belt strapped on, a Northern Arapaho appears primed for action in this photograph taken about 1890. Once relegated to reservations, men who wished to continue as warriors had little choice but to serve as scouts for the army.

The Crow scout Ashishishe—known to whites as Curly—rode with Custer during his ill-fated 1876 expedition against the Sioux resistance leader Sitting Bull.

SETTLING OLD SCORES

The army enlisted Indian scouts from a number of Plains tribes, including warlike groups such as the Comanche, some of whom accepted reservation life and came to terms with the whites. But the bluecoats did their best recruiting among peoples who had fallen on hard times and were threatened by assertive rivals such as the Sioux and their Cheyenne allies—the very tribes most at odds with the army.

Among the scouts who had scores to settle with the Sioux and Cheyenne were Crows from the Montana Territory, Arikaras from the Dakota Territory, and Pawnees from Nebraska. In 1876, when the army called for a company of Pawnee scouts to oppose the defiant Sioux and their allies, 100 men volunteered within an hour. So numerous were the army's native recruits that one Sioux gibed, "Are the Americans afraid to fight themselves, that they hide in a cloud of Indian renegades?"

Comanche scout Essetouyahte made his peace with the soldiers who conducted the campaign along the Washita River in late 1868. Shortly thereafter, he guided Colonel Benjamin Grierson to the site that became Fort Sill—the agency for the Comanche and Kiowa peoples.

The Arikara chief Son of the Star journeyed to Washington, D.C., where this photograph was taken, and pledged to provide scouts for the army's forthcoming campaign against Sitting Bull.

A policeman by the name of Rolling Pony stands proudly with his wife on a reservation in the Indian Territory. For pay of $8 a month, Indian police officers shouldered such duties as halting illicit liquor traffic.

POLICING THE RESERVATION

In 1878, as once-defiant Plains tribes were settling uneasily on reservations, Congress authorized the recruitment of paid Indian police forces at the various agencies. Like the scouts they emulated, these lawmen were following tribal precedent—warrior societies had long maintained order within camp circles. Now, however, the Indian police were often caught between the demands of white agents and the grievances of disaffected tribesmen. Many steered a middle course and kept the peace. Others were drawn into bitter disputes with their own people and came to rue the badge they wore.

This badge was worn by Sioux police officer Bull Head, who led the Indian force sent to arrest Sitting Bull in 1890.

INDIAN POLICE

Mounted patrolmen on the Crow Reservation in Montana evoke the spirit of their tribal predecessors—camp police who were drawn from the ranks of warrior societies such as the Kit Foxes and the Big Dogs.

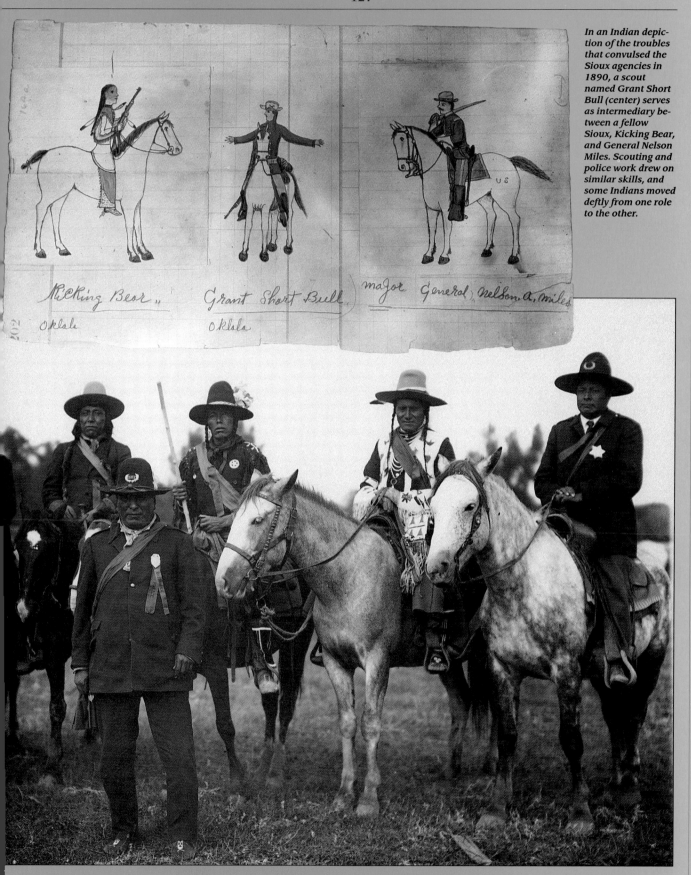

Kicking Bear
Oklala

Grant Short Bull
Oklala

major General, Nelson A. Miles

In an Indian depiction of the troubles that convulsed the Sioux agencies in 1890, a scout named Grant Short Bull (center) serves as intermediary between a fellow Sioux, Kicking Bear, and General Nelson Miles. Scouting and police work drew on similar skills, and some Indians moved deftly from one role to the other.

TRIBESMEN IN UNIFORM

When faced with lingering unrest on the reservations in the early 1890s, the army embraced all-Indian units to bolster the cavalry's peacekeeping efforts. Unlike the scouts of old—who served only as long as they were needed—these volunteers enlisted for five-year terms like white soldiers, and their units were folded into existing regiments. Lieutenant Edward Casey, whose Northern Cheyenne scouts eventually became part of the 8th U.S. Cavalry Regiment, argued that Indians "should have enough distinction to wear a facing of their own," and special trim was designed for their uniforms.

Pride and polish were not enough to preserve the Indian units for long, however. As tensions ebbed at the agencies, top commanders who had been skeptical about the native units from the start mustered them out of the army. Nevertheless, the experiment brought the nation a step closer to accepting Indians as true American soldiers.

A member of a Kiowa troop of the 7th U.S. Cavalry Regiment appears in full dress. The uniform is similar to that designed for Indian scouts at Casey's request (right), which used red and white colors to denote harmony between Indians and whites.

Defying a legacy of bitterness between their tribes and white authorities, Southern Cheyennes and Arapahos inducted into the U.S. Cavalry drill at Fort Reno in the Indian Territory. The recruits are wearing their so-called undress uniform, including a slouch hat.

3

RECKONING AT THE LITTLE BIGHORN

Galloping to the attack, Sioux and Cheyenne warriors overwhelm dismounted cavalrymen in a painting done on deer hide by Cheyenne artist Lame Deer to commemorate the greatest of all Indian victories during the course of the Plains wars—the Battle of the Little Bighorn.

For the Lakota Sioux and their Northern Cheyenne allies, the tall-grass country north of the Bighorn Mountains was a prize worth fighting for. Laced with waterways that carried snowmelt from the heights in the Wyoming Territory down to the Yellowstone River valley in the Montana Territory, the rolling prairie with its lush growth was home to elk, deer, antelope—and buffalo in profusion. The right to hunt here had been purchased in blood from enemy Crow Indians by Lakota and Cheyenne warriors. Now the proud men who were stalking the herds to feed their kin learned that whites meant to force them onto the reservation to the east, where they would lose their freedom and their way of life.

Glimmerings of the trouble ahead reached one of the hunting bands at their winter camp along the Powder River early in 1876. "Soldiers are coming to fight you," a Cheyenne from the reservation told them. The Indians found his words hard to believe. Although some among them had clashed fitfully with whites who ventured too close to their country, their aim was to stay away from the *wasichus,* as the Lakota called the light-skinned intruders, not to confront them. It was difficult to imagine war in such a season. Soon it would be April, a time known to the Lakota as the Moon of the Birth of Calves. Winter was beginning to relax its fierce grip, feeding hopes of better days to come. Buffalo were browsing along the riverbanks; mares were foaling in the pastures. "We were rich, contented, at peace with the whites so far as we knew," recalled a young Cheyenne named Wooden Leg. "Why should soldiers come out to seek for us and fight us?"

To the oncoming bluecoats, however, all Indians who shunned the reservation and held to their old ways were by definition hostile. Approaching from the south was General George Crook, whose force was part of an army expedition aimed at breaking up the camps of the Indians said to be "depredating" east of the Bighorn River in Montana. Deprived of shelter, conventional wisdom held, the survivors would presumably have no choice but to turn to the reservation. Crook, a veteran Indian fighter,

Scores of lodges rise from the rolling prairie along White Clay Creek in South Dakota in an 1891 photograph of a Sioux encampment. In earlier years, free-roaming bands of Sioux, Cheyennes, and other Plains tribes made similar camps on their hunting grounds, always pitching their tipis near fresh water for the people and their ponies.

had set out from Fort Fetterman in Wyoming on the first day of March.

This was unfriendly country for bluecoats, and small war parties harried the soldiers almost from the start. The second night out, a handful of Indians slipped past Crook's pickets to stampede the column's 45 cattle, greatly depleting the meat ration for Crook's 12 companies. For the duration of the campaign, the 785 officers, enlisted men, muleteers, and scouts would have to subsist on coffee, hardtack, and some rancid bacon. Three nights after that, with the bivouac lighted by lanterns and campfires, warriors sent the soldiers into a near panic by peppering them with gunfire for more than half an hour. And for the next 10 days, Crook's hungry troopers were shadowed by Indians as they groped morosely northward through snow squalls to the vicinity of the Powder River in southeastern Montana.

The hunting band to which Wooden Leg belonged had scouts out watching for the soldiers. But on the wickedly cold night of March 16, they lost contact—just as an attack force of 375 men sent ahead by Crook under the command of Colonel Joseph Reynolds was nearing their camp. Pitched along the Powder River were some 60 Cheyenne and 40 Lakota tipis, sheltering nearly 700 people in all.

As cavalrymen descended the slopes toward the camp in the dawn light, no alarm rose from the village. Feeling secure in the abilities of their scouts and loath to face the biting cold, the villagers dozed on, wrapped in buffalo robes. Then an old man left his lodge and climbed a knoll to pray. "The soldiers are right here! The soldiers are right here!" he screamed.

Down through the village galloped the first company of 47 cavalrymen, yelling and firing their pistols. Behind them came other companies to cut out the Indians' pony herd and lend support. The opening cavalry charge caused more commotion than harm, and as the soldiers re-formed to storm back through the lodges, warriors rallied. Throwing off their robes, they reached for their guns, bows, and knives; slashed their way out of their securely fastened tipis; and stepped out into the chill air wearing little or nothing. There was no stopping the bluecoats from marauding through the village, so the men retreated with their women and children to the safety of nearby brush and timber. Then they turned and fired on the soldiers, forcing troopers to dismount and scramble for cover. A few of them did not make it. Wooden Leg was drawing his bow when the warrior beside him shot a soldier with a muzzleloading rifle. "We rushed upon the man and beat and stabbed him to death," Wooden Leg recalled. "I stripped off the blue coat and kept it."

In all, the warriors killed four soldiers and wounded six, while suffering only a few casualties of their own. Although Reynolds's men were supposed to hold the village until Crook arrived with the remainder of his force, the resistance so surprised the colonel that he ordered the soldiers to withdraw after destroying the camp. They carried away what food they could, then put lodges to the torch, depriving the Indians of shelter, provisions, and precious keepsakes.

The villagers were stung by the loss, but they regained hope that night when a party of their warriors crept close to the soldiers' camp and retrieved hundreds of ponies taken from them during the attack. With their mobility restored, they sought refuge among bands of the Oglala and Hunkpapa Sioux, branches of the Lakota. The fugitives spent three bitter nights in the open before arriving at the hunting camp of the great Oglala warrior Crazy Horse, whose people generously offered them food and shelter. At a council, the newcomers told of the recent attack, and both bands decided to hurry on to a large village of Hunkpapas, led by a chief renowned for his refusal to bow to the demands of the wasichus—Sitting Bull. At the village, the refugees were embraced like family. "A 10-year-old Hunkpapa girl put a buffalo robe in front of me," Wooden Leg recalled. "It was mine now. A Hunkpapa man gave my father a medicine pipe to replace his lost one. Oh, what good hearts they had. I never can forget the generosity of Sitting Bull's Hunkpapa Sioux on that day."

Listening to the refugees tell of their ordeal, Sitting Bull understood that a confrontation was near. "These soldiers have come shooting. They want war," he said. "We must stand together or they will kill us separately."

Faced with such a challenge, the Lakota and their Cheyenne allies were fortunate to have leaders of the caliber of Sitting Bull and Crazy Horse. In some ways, the two could not have been more different. Crazy Horse, now in his mid-thirties, was a brilliant and brooding war chief who disdained the taking of scalps and seldom spoke in councils. Sitting Bull, roughly 10 years older, reveled in rousing oratory. Yet Crazy Horse and Sitting Bull were united by a sense of mission. Both were holy men who drew strength from visions and rituals and regarded confinement to the reservation as a threat not just to the prosperity of the Lakota but to their sacred traditions. To surrender the hunting grounds, they believed, was to lose the power granted to the people by the spirits of the creatures they pursued. Such power resounded in the very name of Sitting Bull—a title he inherited from his father after proving his bravery as an adolescent. The name evoked the proud image of a buffalo bull on its haunches, sturdy and implacable.

Sitting Bull, pictured below in the early 1880s, kept the sacred buffalo skull at left with him during his struggle with pursuing troops in 1876 and invoked the animal's protective spirit in ceremonies.

A MAN OF THE PEOPLE

From a young age, Sitting Bull showed the strength and generosity expected of a Lakota chief. At 10, he killed his first buffalo calf, donating the meat to the poor who had no horses. At 14, he counted his first coup in battle. Thereafter he earned many honors: membership in the Strong Heart warrior society; recognition as a *wichasha wakan,* or holy man; and appointment as supreme chief of the Lakotas and Cheyennes who shunned the reservations.

For all his distinctions, however, Sitting Bull personified the simple virtues of the hunter-warriors who followed him. Like them, he enjoyed nothing so much as recounting his exploits—in words, in song, and in drawings. And as they did, he took great pride in the large family he supported. Before the Battle of the Little Bighorn in 1876, he shared his lodge with no fewer than a dozen dependents, including his mother, two wives, and seven children.

Sitting Bull celebrated his deeds in a series of drawings, many of which were copied and preserved by his uncle Chief Four Horns. Here, Sitting Bull counts his first coup as a youth. In honor of the feat, he received his father's name—Sitting Bull—which inspired the buffalo symbol used here to identify him (upper right).

Wearing the horn headdress and other battle attire of the Strong Heart warrior society, Sitting Bull depicts himself killing a Crow chief. In the Lakota tradition, this act endowed him with the slain man's qualities and earned him the rank of war chief.

Sitting Bull takes charge of a young Assiniboin captured during a clash with that tribe in 1857. Adopted by Sitting Bull, who named him Jumping Bull, the captive was one of several young men the chief took into his large family.

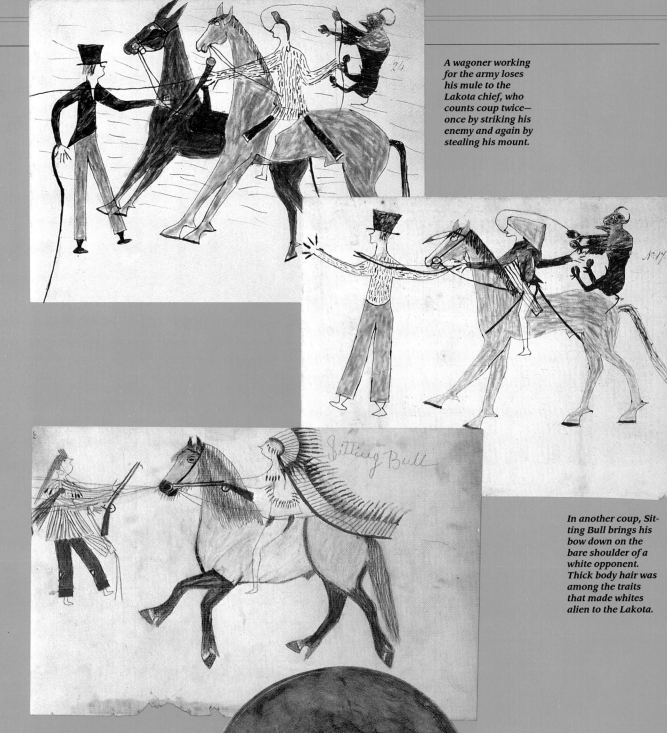

A wagoner working for the army loses his mule to the Lakota chief, who counts coup twice—once by striking his enemy and again by stealing his mount.

In another coup, Sitting Bull brings his bow down on the bare shoulder of a white opponent. Thick body hair was among the traits that made whites alien to the Lakota.

Sitting Bull

Pursued by an Indian serving as an army scout, Sitting Bull turns on his foe and shoots him before the scout is able to fire his rifle.

Besides drawings, Sitting Bull composed songs for ceremonies. This drum was among his prized possessions.

Along with an army officer's wife, Sitting Bull appears with one of his wives and four of his children outside of their lodge at Fort Randall in the Dakota Territory, where the chief was detained by federal authorities after returning from Canada.

Among his many natural children— including two sets of twins—Sitting Bull was especially fond of his son Crow Foot (near right), born three weeks before the Little Bighorn battle; and his daughter Standing Holy (far right), who was born two years later when Sitting Bull had taken refuge in Canada.

One of Sitting Bull's pipes bears his autograph on the stem. He learned to sign his name during his time in Canada.

Between them, Crazy Horse and Sitting Bull had been present at many of the major clashes between the Lakota and wasichus during the quarter century since tribes of the Plains first gathered at Fort Laramie and agreed to keep the peace with each other and with the whites. Sitting Bull's Hunkpapa—one of seven branches of the Lakota—avoided that 1851 conclave and spurned the treaty. Sitting Bull came of age believing that he and his fellow warriors had the right and the duty to challenge such traditional rivals as the Crow, the Shoshone, and the Arikara, as well as any wasichus who dared to defy them.

Crazy Horse, for his part, was said to have witnessed the incident in 1854 that shattered the peace around Fort Laramie—Lieutenant John Grattan's rash attempt to punish a young Lakota for killing a stray cow. About 13 years old at the time, he and some of his Oglala kin were camped with an allied band of Brulé Sioux when the incident occurred. Grattan's attack and the furious response of the Brulé warriors set the stage for an experience that transformed the boy. After the fighting, he left his companions and embarked on a vision quest. Following several days of self-inflicted pain, he fell into a trance and dreamed of a warrior who bore haunting signs of spirit power. Years later, when he reached fighting age, Crazy Horse told of his vision and entered battle thereafter like the warrior in the dream—with a lightning streak painted on his face, hail marks inscribed on his body, and the skin of a red-backed hawk in his hair.

Crazy Horse's Oglala branch occupied the lower reaches of Lakota territory, extending southward from the Powder River country near the Montana-Wyoming border to the emigrant trails along the North Platte River. Sitting Bull's Hunkpapas made their camps farther north, from the Yellowstone River eastward along the upper Missouri River—a position that embroiled the young chief and his followers in clashes with white troops that grew out of the conflict with Little Crow's Dakotas in 1862. As Dakotas fled westward from Minnesota along with disaffected Yanktonai Sioux, Sitting Bull and other northern Lakota war leaders joined forces with them, and together they opposed troops sent to "pacify" the Sioux. The allied Indian war parties suffered a series of setbacks, culminating in July of 1864 at Killdeer Mountain along the Little Missouri River, where Sitting Bull found that the Sioux with their penchant for acts of individual daring were no match for cohesive army units with superior firepower. Henceforth, he sought better weapons for his warriors and picked his fights carefully, harrying soldiers around their forts and ambushing intruding parties of settlers, prospectors, and surveyors.

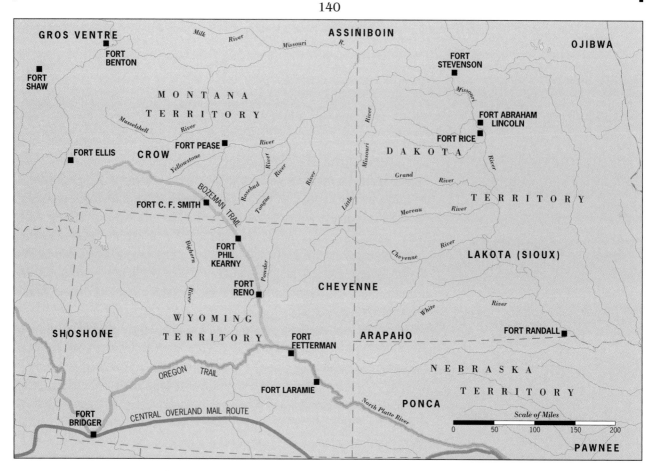

Crazy Horse, meanwhile, was providing a mighty assist to the defiant Oglala chief Red Cloud in his campaign to drive Montana-bound miners and their military protectors from the prized Powder River country. In December 1866 at Fort Phil Kearny in northern Wyoming, Crazy Horse demonstrated that the bluecoats could indeed be bested if the Indians relied on the raider's age-old tactics of deception and surprise. In a classic decoy, he lured Captain William Fetterman and his force of 80 men into pursuing what Fetterman thought was a small band of hostile Indians. Once exposed, the bluecoats were surrounded by hundreds of warriors and annihilated. For the army, the so-called Fetterman Massacre was a shocking debacle. General Sherman proposed that the hostile bands "be punished with vindictive earnestness until at least 10 Indians are killed for each white life lost." But Congress worried that further clashes with Indians on the Northern Plains would imperil westward expansion and instead dispatched peacemakers to negotiate with Red Cloud and other defiant leaders in the region. In 1868 chiefs once again traveled to Fort Laramie to ratify a new accord.

The terms of that treaty—which covered six pages of fine print—were not easily grasped by the chiefs, who had to rely on interpreters. Ignoring the daunting diversity of the Sioux with their many branches, the treaty established a single Great Sioux Reservation, covering the western half of present-day South Dakota (much of which would later be infringed on by

By the spring of 1876, a showdown was near in the long-simmering conflict between the U.S. Army—whose troops were stationed at forts across the Northern Plains to protect white settlers and travelers—and defiant Sioux, Cheyenne, and Arapaho hunting bands, who occupied the Powder River country of southeastern Montana. With the help of Indians hostile to the Sioux and Cheyenne, including Crows and Shoshones, the army set out to destroy the camps of the bands and force them onto reservations.

white settlers and prospectors). Little of that was prime hunting ground; the Indians would have to rely largely on government issue rations and whatever they could raise through the farming techniques that agents promised to teach them. In a concession to Red Cloud, the treaty defined the Powder River country as "unceded territory." There Indians might continue to hunt, the document declared, "for as long as the buffalo range." It was a fine promise, but the treaty also stipulated that the Sioux relinquish their right to permanently occupy any land off the reservation. Presumably, their right to the unceded territory would expire when the buffalo were hunted out. But long before that, officials would invoke this deceptive clause as grounds for forcing all Sioux onto the reservation.

The treaty succeeded in driving a wedge through the Lakota peoples. Red Cloud honored it, but Crazy Horse wanted nothing to do with the whites or their reservation and became champion of the so-called nontreaty Oglalas. Other Lakota branches were similarly divided. Some Indians straddled the fence, living on the reservation in the winter and ranging abroad to hunt in the summer. But roughly one-third of the Lakota population ignored the wasichus and their legalities and roamed freely as they had before. Among the Hunkpapa, only a lower-ranking chief named Gall traveled to Fort Laramie, and Sitting Bull's followers paid no heed to the strange document he affixed his mark to.

A year or so after the conclave at Fort Laramie, Indians who rejected the treaty and spurned reservation life gathered along Rosebud Creek in southeastern Montana and acknowledged Sitting Bull as their principal chief. Among those joining his Hunkpapas for the occasion were Oglalas, Miniconjous, Sans Arcs, and Northern Cheyennes—who had grown so close to the Lakota that they were virtually a part of them. Never before among the fiercely independent Sioux had such a diverse assembly recognized one man above all others. Sitting Bull's authority was limited: He did not have the right to command the obedience of other leaders or their followers. Yet his powers of persuasion were such that he exercised considerable influence over them.

Crazy Horse, who cared little for such honors, was content to lend his clout as a war chief to the loose alliance Sitting Bull now presided over. The nontreaty Lakotas would need the talents of both men, for new threats were emerging that would test their resolve. By the summer of 1871, surveyors for the Northern Pacific Railroad were poking westward through Lakota hunting grounds along the Yellowstone River accompanied by army escorts. When Sitting Bull called on his warriors to resist this

imposition, the whites invited him to yet another parley. Sitting Bull sent his brother-in-law to say that he would be happy to talk, "whenever he found a white man who would tell the truth."

Three years later, the Lakota were further angered when Lieutenant Colonel George Armstrong Custer, who had earlier commanded the assault on Black Kettle's camp at Washita, led a federal expedition into the Black Hills and found gold there. Soon prospectors were flocking to the area, encroaching on ground that had been set aside for the Sioux by treaty and that was prized by Indians both on and off the reservation.

This new gold rush stiffened the spine of Sitting Bull and his followers even as it placed fresh pressure on federal authorities to end resistance among the Sioux and make the region safe for white fortune seekers. In

April 1875, President Ulysses S. Grant, with a bluntness reminiscent of his days as a Union general, laid down the law to a delegation of Sioux and Cheyennes summoned from the reservation to Washington. "White people outnumber the Indians at least 200 to one," Grant informed his guests. Should the Indians be so foolish as to resort to hostilities, he added, the government would necessarily withhold their meat rations, which after all were simply gratuities that "could be taken from them at any time."

Leaving the reservation Indians to ponder the threat of starvation, Grant next approved military action against the so-called hostiles still roaming free. As in earlier campaigns on the Southern Plains, the objective of this operation, as one official put it confidentially, was to catch the defiant Indians in their winter camps "and whip them into subjection." Toward year's end, messengers were sent to the hunting bands camped northeast of the Bighorn Mountains to warn them to report to the agencies by January 31, 1876, or face the consequences—a request that must have seemed strange indeed to people who lived by a lunar calendar and seldom ventured far in the depths of winter. None of the bands complied.

Operational orders for the campaign were cut in February. The plan

General William Tecumseh Sherman (above, with jacket unbuttoned) looks on intently as Indian chiefs consider the terms of the peace treaty negotiated at Fort Laramie in 1868. At right, an Oglala Sioux chieftain named Man Afraid of His Horses puffs on a council pipe amid other Indian delegates to the conference.

called for three columns to converge on the winter camps. General Crook would head north from Wyoming's Fort Fetterman; Colonel John Gibbon would move east from Fort Ellis in central Montana; and Brigadier General Alfred Terry would march west from Fort Abraham Lincoln in the Dakota Territory with a force that included Custer's 7th U.S. Cavalry Regiment. Swelling the three columns would be scores of Indian scouts and fighting auxiliaries drawn from the ranks of the Crow, Shoshone, and other tribes at odds with the Lakota and the Northern Cheyenne. The War Department was confident that the converging columns would soon bring the hostiles to bay, for officers persisted in believing that Indians would not stand up to massed firepower. No one was more attached to that idea than Custer.

Nevertheless, several factors conspired to make the war parties that were gathered around Sitting Bull among the toughest opponents the U.S. Army had ever targeted on the Plains. Sitting Bull had cultivated strong ties with traders, and his men were thus well stocked with ammunition and firearms, including repeating rifles. Relations between the defiant hunting bands were close, improving the chances for coordination in battle. Repeated clashes with whites and rival Indian tribes in recent years had accustomed both the warriors and their kin to conflict; women urged their men to be brave and eagerly assisted them on the warpath, while boys yearned to apply the predatory skills they had been honing in games and on the hunt. Above all, the Indians were fueled by a conviction that few white soldiers had shared since the end of the crusade called the Civil War: They believed that their cause was sacred and that eternal spirits would strengthen their hand in battle and bring them glory.

The army officers had more than defiant Indians to contend with. Harsh conditions on the Northern Plains—where snow, ice, and mud bedeviled travelers well into the spring—played havoc with their plans. Only Crook's force managed to get under way in March, and the lone attack his men carried out against the Powder River camp at midmonth merely served to put the Indians on their guard. Afterward, Crook withdrew to Fort Fetterman and regrouped. It was May before circumstances permitted a resumption of the campaign on all three fronts.

In the meantime, warriors and their kin were rallying around Sitting Bull. After fugitives from the Powder River assault arrived at Sitting Bull's village, messengers galloped off to warn other roaming bands in the area of the impending threat. Before long, 55 lodges of Miniconjou Sioux under their chief Lame Deer arrived to join the 250 lodges of Hunkpapas,

The proud Oglala Sioux chief Red Cloud wears a presidential medal and holds a peace pipe in a picture taken after he signed the 1868 Fort Laramie treaty and gave up fighting. Determined to halt traffic on the Bozeman Trail through Oglala hunting grounds, Red Cloud had repeatedly attacked the forts along the route and agreed to peace only after the army abandoned them. "When we see the soldiers moving away," he declared, "then I will come down and talk."

Oglalas, and Northern Cheyennes already assembled there. Scattered bands followed, including Lakotas of the Brulé, Sans Arc, and Blackfeet branches, along with some Yanktonais and even a few persevering Dakotas from Minnesota.

The neighboring camp circles of the various bands grew to include more than 460 lodges. All together they sheltered about 4,000 Indians, including more than 1,000 warriors. The forest of tipis extended for miles, and all around milled vast herds of horses—up to 20,000 animals in all. The grazing ponies stripped the neighboring hillsides of growth even as the hunters exhausted local supplies of game, forcing the Indians to move their camp every few days. Following the buffalo, they edged westward from the Powder River, crossing the Tongue River in May and reaching Rosebud Creek by early June.

At their meetings, warriors renewed their pledge to resist the wasichus. "One after another of my warriors rose and counseled war," recalled the Cheyenne chief Two Moons. "We wanted our revenge."

Yet Sitting Bull and other leaders discouraged attacks on the wasichus, hoping that their opponents might lose heart if they were not provoked. "We supposed," said Wooden Leg, "that the combined camps would frighten off the soldiers. We hoped thus to be freed of their annoyance."

The soldiers were not easily put off, however. In May, before setting out again from Fort Fetterman, General Crook had sought help in recruiting Lakotas for his campaign from the Oglala leader Red Cloud. The old chief had long since made his peace with the whites. But he would do nothing to help Crook or hurt those Oglalas who had joined forces with Sitting Bull—a group that included one of the chief's own sons. Red Cloud reportedly told Crook that the Sioux "have many warriors, many guns and ponies. They are brave and ready to fight for their country. They are not afraid of the soldiers or of their chief. Every lodge will send its young men, and they all will say of the Great Father's dogs, 'Let them come.'"

Crook got under way on May 29 without a single Lakota recruit, but with the hope of enticing Crows and Shoshones from their reservations as he made his way northward. By now the other two columns were at last on the march. Such large movements could not be concealed, and word of their approach soon reached Sitting Bull, prompting the chief and his followers to make spiritual preparations as well as military ones.

Each year when Lakota hunting bands came together for their summer encampment, devout men joined in the solemn Sun Dance to acknowledge the blessings that sustained the tribe by offering their flesh and blood to the supreme spirit they called Wakan Tanka, or the Great Mystery. For Sitting Bull, the ritual this year had a special urgency; his people were confronted with a fearsome challenge, and their need for spiritual support had never been greater. Toward the beginning of June, he prayed on behalf of his followers to Wakan Tanka, asking for divine assistance and promising in return to give of himself at the Sun Dance. Only Hunkpapas joined their chief in the ceremony that followed. But throngs from all the camp circles crowded around to observe.

True to his pledge, Sitting Bull offered Wakan Tanka a "scarlet blanket"—an offering of his own blood. It was an ordeal he had undergone before, as livid scars on his back and chest attested. Fellow holy men painted Sitting Bull's hands and feet red, and drew blue stripes across his shoulders. Then he sat with his back to the sacred dance pole, chanting prayers, while his adopted brother, Jumping Bull, knelt before him with an awl in one hand and a knife in the other. Starting at Sitting Bull's right wrist, Jumping Bull inserted the awl, lifted a bit of flesh, and sliced it off with the knife. Blood purled from the wound. Working with swift precision, Jumping Bull moved up his brother's arm to the shoulder, inflicting 50 gouges in all. No signs of pain marred Sitting Bull's prayers. Jumping Bull turned to the left arm and again made 50 cuts from wrist to shoulder. At last the chief held out his offering to Wakan Tanka—a scarlet blanket covering his arms and flowing in rivulets from his steady hands.

Sitting Bull rose. Facing the sun and staring at the burning orb, he began to dance while he prayed on. To avoid going blind, Sitting Bull from

More than 1,000 troops and civilians, along with about 100 supply wagons, wind through a pass in the Black Hills during Lieutenant Colonel George Armstrong Custer's 1874 reconnaissance into this rugged corner of the Dakota Territory, reserved for the Sioux under the Fort Laramie treaty. Reports from Custer's expedition of gold in the hills brought thousands of miners to the area in defiance of the treaty.

time to time lowered his focus to the rim of the sun, but he met its glare steadily, agonizingly. The dance and the prayers continued through the night and into the next day. Then about noon, Sitting Bull halted with his eyes toward the sun as if transfixed.

The vision he sought came to him with blinding clarity. White soldiers were descending like grasshoppers on a distant Indian village. But they were upside down, with their heads to the ground. They were falling into the camp not as conquerors but as dead men.

In the midst of this revelation, Sitting Bull lapsed into unconsciousness; some Lakotas would say that he died a passing death. When he revived, he spoke of his vision, and joy spread through the camp. The followers of Sitting Bull felt certain now that they were destined for victory.

Their confidence would soon be put to the test. Once again, it was Crook's column that would mount the first challenge. By June 9, his force of more than 1,000 men had reached the Tongue River near the Wyoming-Montana border, where they paused to await recruits from the reservations. Several days later, those auxiliaries arrived in force—86 Shoshones and 175 Crows. For the Crows, it was a chance to strike back at rivals who had driven them from this fine hunting ground.

Crook's teeming bivouac along the Tongue River did not go unnoticed. Among the Indians who spotted the soldiers there were Wooden Leg and other members of a Cheyenne hunting band, who had ventured out from the Rosebud encampment in pursuit of buffalo and ended up trailing bluecoats. Early one morning, Wooden Leg recalled, they spied a reconnaissance force of about 20 Indians riding from the soldier camp: "Were they Crows? Were they Shoshones? We exchanged guesses, but we did not know." The Cheyennes were tempted to attack the Indians and count coup, but thought better of it. "We considered it most important that we return and notify our people on the Rosebud," Wooden Leg recalled. "We saw soldiers walking about their camp. It had been flooded by the high waters. They were splashing about here and there and appeared to be getting ready to travel. We decided it was time for us also to travel."

Crook's men moved out in the direction of the Rosebud on June 15, but the Cheyennes were ahead of them. On their way back to the camp, Wooden Leg and his hungry mates killed a buffalo, but they had no time to relish it. "We quickly divided up the liver and ate the raw segments," he recollected. "Over a hastily built fire, we toasted little chunks of buffalo meat. As we devoured them, we spoke but few words. Whatever speech was uttered was in jerky sputterings. Everybody was excited. Every minute or two somebody was jumping up to go somewhere and look for pursuing soldiers. After the food had been bolted, we hastened to move on." Soon they reached the encampment and warned of the approaching force: "We wolf-howled and aroused the people. Some Sioux were there and they carried the news to their people. Soon all the camp circles were in a fever of excitement. Heralds were riding about and shouting: 'Soldiers have been seen. They are coming in this direction. Indians are with them.'"

The Sioux and Cheyennes promptly decamped and moved westward toward the Little Bighorn River through a divide in the low ridge known as the Wolf Mountains. They left behind a band of scouts led by a Cheyenne named Little Hawk to watch for the soldiers. By nightfall on June 16, General Crook had reached the Rosebud some distance south of the recently abandoned campsite. Little Hawk brought word of the enemy presence to the chiefs that evening, and they resolved to remain on the defensive. "Leave the soldiers alone unless they attack us," they told their warriors. But the war fever that was building among the young men could not be contained. Hundreds of them rode off impulsively in the night to challenge the bluecoats, and Sitting Bull and Crazy Horse hastened to back them up.

Early the next morning, June 17, Crook learned from his scouts that there were signs of hostiles in the distance to the north, and his men headed off in that direction along the Rosebud. A few hours later, they stopped to rest: Crook ordered his cavalry to dismount and unsaddle, and sent some Crows and Shoshones ahead to probe for opposition. Those auxiliaries were wary, but Crook and his men remained unperturbed, for the Sioux and Cheyennes had shown no signs of seeking a fight. An hour later, the general was engrossed in a game of whist and his men were sipping coffee when the distant sound of firing rolled down the valley. "They are shooting buffaloes over there," remarked an officer, thinking that the auxiliaries—who had pursued game the day before—were once more on the hunt. But soon the reverberations grew louder. Suddenly, Crows raced in from the north screaming, "Lakota! Lakota!" Fast upon their wake came hundreds of mounted warriors, sweeping down on the lounging soldiers.

While the troopers scrambled to saddle up, the Crows and Shoshones rallied and met the onslaught, breaking the surge. Soon the bluecoats weighed in and pushed the attackers back, but the Sioux and Cheyennes continued to swarm about, launching charge after charge. To the soldiers, the Indians were dreadful in their appearance and daunting in their horse-

Surprised by Sioux and Cheyenne warriors at the Battle of the Rosebud on June 17, 1876, General George Crook later withdrew southward to await reinforcements, leaving it to other army columns to deal with the defiant bands.

manship. Captain Anson Mills described them as "painted in most hideous colors and designs, stark naked except for their moccasins, breech clouts, and head gear." Yet these unseemly opponents, Mills added, "were the best cavalry on earth. In charging towards us, they exposed little of their person, hanging on with one arm around the neck and one leg over the horse, firing and lancing from underneath the horses' necks so that there was no part of the Indians at which we could aim."

As the battle seesawed back and forth, a Cheyenne warrior named Comes in Sight had his mount shot out from under him. He was afoot and facing certain death at the hands of the Crows. But as his enemies closed in, a lone rider came zigzagging through the fray. Reaching down, the rider locked arms with the beleaguered warrior and helped him swing up on the pony's rump. The two raced off to safety through a hail of bullets. The Cheyennes later revealed that the rescuer was none other than Comes in Sight's own sister, Buffalo Calf Road Woman. Tribal tradition celebrated the Rosebud fight as the battle Where the Girl Saved Her Brother.

After several hours of fighting, Crook's force seemed to have the situation in hand. Suspecting that the enemy lodges were nearby, Crook felt confident enough to detach roughly half his command—eight companies of cavalry—and send them off in search of the encampment. Once they departed, the remaining units had to consolidate their forces, and the Sioux and Cheyennes seized the opportunity and launched a thunderous charge. As many as 500 mounted warriors assailed cavalrymen on Crook's left flank before they could close ranks with the main formation. In the ensuing melee, some bluecoats lost their mounts and had to wield their carbines as clubs in hand-to-hand combat. Crook responded by shifting two infantry companies to the crumbling flank. Once again in a

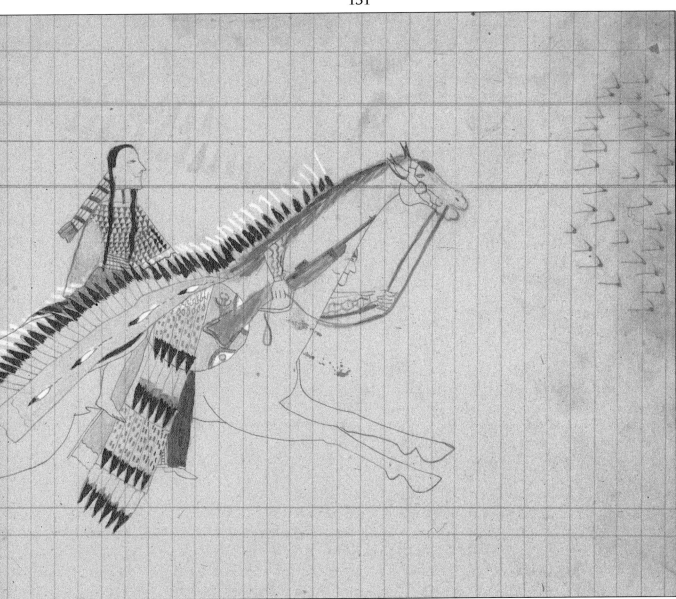

General Crook's blue-coated troops fire in vain on the Cheyenne heroine of the Battle of the Rosebud, Buffalo Calf Road Woman, who gallops off after rescuing her brother, Chief Comes in Sight—shown draped over the far side of the horse, with a rifle in his right hand and his shield and war bonnet hanging behind. The picture was painted in a ledger by a Northern Cheyenne artist.

close contest between soldiers and Indians, superior army firepower turned the tide. Troopers who escaped with their lives gave credit as well to the Crows and Shoshones, who formed a stout defensive line behind which many of them found refuge.

Amid the crisis, Crook sent his adjutant to recall the companies searching for the Indian encampment. The adjutant found them probing a narrow canyon and delivered his message: Crook was hard pressed; he needed them. Following expert Indian guides, the soldiers worked their way out of the canyon, circled wide around the battlefield, and came up on the flank and rear of the Sioux and Cheyennes who, weary after six hours of fighting, promptly disengaged. The Battle of the Rosebud was over.

Crook counted 10 men killed and 21 wounded. Crazy Horse—who had been in the thick of the fighting as usual, urging his warriors on—later put the losses among the Indians at more than 30 killed and 60 wounded, a tally that reflected a keen spirit of sacrifice among war parties that under normal circumstances sought to keep casualties to a minimum. Crook claimed victory because he had remained on the battlefield and his foes had departed. Yet the strength and determination of the opposition left him wary. He was low on rations and ammunition after the battle and decided that he could not resume the offensive until his men had been resupplied and their ranks bolstered by the 5th U.S. Cavalry Regiment, which was busy elsewhere coping with restive Cheyennes and would not arrive for several weeks. Crook withdrew, taking his forces to encamp along Goose Creek, a tributary of the Tongue River in Wyoming. Thus Sitting Bull's followers had achieved a coup. Not only had they shielded their encampment from imminent attack but they had sidetracked the strongest of the forces sent to subdue them. When the Indians next fought bluecoats, Crook and his able auxiliaries would be out of the picture.

After the battle, the Sioux and Cheyennes settled in along the Little Bighorn River. Buoyed by their success in fending off Crook's troopers, they soon found further cause for celebration as large bands began arriving from the Sioux and Cheyenne reservations to swell their encampment. It was not the first time that Indians had migrated from the agencies in June to pursue buffalo and supplement their government rations. But this year, the so-called summer roamers had more than hunting on their mind. They were aggrieved by the Black Hills gold rush and by the threat from the Great Father to withhold their beef rations if they reacted. They knew of the attack on the Powder River camp in March and resented such attempts to drive hunting bands from the area. If bluecoats threatened them, they were prepared to strike back.

Among the fresh arrivals were contingents of Hunkpapas under Chiefs Gall and Crow King, who came to support their militant kinsmen: 120 lodges of Oglalas; 50 lodges of Brulés; and untold numbers of Cheyennes. Within a week, the encampment had doubled in size to nearly 1,000 lodges, sheltering at least 1,800 warriors. Never before had so many Indian fighting men joined forces on the Plains.

The troopers pursuing these warriors had little idea of what they were up against. On June 21, the commanders of the two columns converging on the area from west and east—Colonel Gibbon and General Terry—met aboard the steamboat *Far West* at the confluence of the Rosebud and the Yellowstone. As the superior officer, Terry took charge of the operation. He

Horsemen wearing war bonnets ford the clear waters of the Little Bighorn during a 1909 peace council held at the famous battle site. In mid-June of 1876, Sioux and Cheyenne hunting bands arrived on this site following the clash with Crook's forces along the Rosebud and pitched their camps on the west bank of the Little Bighorn.

had yet to receive word of Crook's encounter with the Indians on the Rosebud four days previously. Terry was forced to rely solely on the intelligence provided by Gibbon's Crow scouts and by a recent reconnaissance led by Major Marcus Reno of the 7th Cavalry. Their reports indicated that an encampment of hostile Indians—thought to number about 400 lodges and 800 warriors—had recently left the vicinity of Rosebud Creek and moved westward toward the Little Bighorn.

Unaware that the encampment there was growing larger by the day, Terry concluded that the 600 men of Custer's 7th Cavalry could overpower the opposition. The general outlined his plan of attack: Custer would move southward up the Rosebud, cut westward to the headwaters of the Little Bighorn River, and then sweep north along that waterway toward its confluence with the Bighorn, where Gibbon's smaller column would set up a blocking position. With any luck, Custer would smash the encampment along the Little Bighorn, and Gibbon would corral the fugitives. Terry himself would travel with Gibbon.

Colonel Gibbon suspected that Custer, still youthfully impulsive at 36,

A lounging George Armstrong Custer studies a map at an army camp in 1873 with his favorite Indian scout, the Arikara Bloody Knife (to Custer's right), while other scouts look on. Bloody Knife, whom Custer referred to as "my brother," accompanied the colonel during his Black Hills expedition and joined him again for his 1876 campaign. Ignoring Bloody Knife's warnings of trouble ahead, Custer hurried his men into battle at the Little Bighorn with flags flying, including the guidon above.

would hurry his men along and attack before Gibbon's blocking force could get into position, which might take four days. "Now don't be greedy, Custer," Gibbon wryly admonished his younger colleague before they parted on June 22. "There are enough Indians for all of us. Wait for us." Yet that seemed a faint hope to others who knew Custer. Wrote Lieutenant James Bradley, Gibbon's chief of scouts: "It is understood that if Custer arrives first, he is at liberty to attack if he deems prudent. We have little hope of being in at the death, as Custer undoubtedly will exert himself to win all the laurels for himself and his regiment."

The column that wound southward from the Yellowstone under Custer numbered 31 officers, 585 enlisted men, 14 civilians, and 36 Indian scouts—mostly Arikaras and Crows. Custer was offered a battery of .50-caliber Gatling guns, but rejected it as too cumbersome; he would be chasing Indians, not fighting pitched battles with them.

By June 24, his force had reached the abandoned campsite along the Rosebud where Sitting Bull had performed the Sun Dance. Left behind there were signs that made the scouts apprehensive. An Arikara called Red Star later told of pictographs drawn in the dirt portraying dead soldiers, of a buffalo calfskin tied to four upright sticks, and of other symbols charged with Sitting Bull's potent medicine. Some scouts interpreted them as bad omens for Custer, but they carried on.

More alarming still was the message the scouts were able to read in the tracks of their quarry. The earlier markings of a large encampment were overlaid with more recent lodgepole trails and the detritus of many smaller camps; here and there, the scouts found horse droppings that were only a few days old. Custer fretted that the hostiles might be scattering, but the scouts suspected the truth: After Sitting Bull's people decamped, a fresh influx of Indians had paused here and then continued on to join the main force. A mixed-blood scout named Mitch Bouyer had been saying all along, "We are going to have a damn big fight." Now Custer's favorite scout, a graying Arikara named Bloody Knife, warned that more enemies lay ahead than there were bullets in the belts of the soldiers. Later, Bloody Knife told Custer, "We'll find enough Sioux to keep fighting two or three days." To which Custer replied coolly, "Oh, I guess we'll get through with them in one day."

On one issue, there could be no debate: The tracks revealed that the Indians camped here had headed west toward the Little Bighorn through the divide in the Wolf Mountains. That discovery led Custer to a fateful decision. General Terry, fearing that the 7th Cavalry would collide with the

Cheyenne chief Two Moons wears a magnificent headdress trimmed with ermine pendants in a portrait taken about 1900 by photographer Edward Curtis. After an encampment of Northern Cheyennes was attacked by General Crook in March of 1876, an angry Two Moons joined forces with Sitting Bull and led his warriors against federal troops at the Battles of the Rosebud and the Little Bighorn.

hostile encampment before Gibbon was in place, had earlier urged Custer to avoid any such shortcut and take the long route around the southern end of the ridge. With the hostiles seemingly in his grasp, however, Custer ignored those instructions and sent his men hurrying up the divide that very evening. After midnight, they halted in a wooded ravine, while the scouts proceeded up a hill known as the Crow's Nest, which afforded a fine view of the surrounding countryside. As dawn broke on June 25, the keenest-eyed scouts could make out the distant forms of pony herds, undulating like worms along the Little Bighorn almost 15 miles away. The Indian encampment itself was out of sight—but the presence of so many horses betrayed its size and proximity.

A short while later, Custer himself rode up to the Crow's Nest to have a look, but he could see nothing. In the midst of such uncertainty, he considered putting off his attack until after Gibbon had had an opportunity to set up his blocking position on the following day, June 26. But Custer soon learned that his men's presence had been discovered. A group of Sioux warriors had been seen prowling close by, and now an alarming report arrived that Indians had been spotted farther back on the trail, rummaging among a load of hardtack that a mule had bucked off in the night. Fearing above all that his quarry would sense his approach and flee, Custer chose to forge ahead. Still ignorant of the magnitude of the opposition, he hurried his men down the dusty trail in full daylight, leaving the packtrain with its ammunition reserves to follow them at a slower pace.

It was a quiet morning in the vast encampment along the west bank of the Little Bighorn. The night before, warriors had joined in festive dances after venturing out after buffalo, and today many of them slept late in their lodges while women turned out early to dry the buffalo meat or forage for roots or berries. About midday, a Lakota war leader named Runs the Enemy was smoking his pipe with a few other men in his camp circle when some visiting Sioux who had recently left the village hurried back to report

The army's 1876 campaign called for three columns to converge on Sitting Bull and his followers in southeastern Montana. One column headed north from Wyoming under Crook—and pulled back after being battered along the Rosebud. A second column led by Colonel John Gibbon moved eastward, while a third headed west from the Dakota Territory under Brigadier General Alfred Terry and his subordinate Custer. At a rendezvous on the Yellowstone, Terry—unaware of the opposition's strength—divided his forces, ordering Gibbon to approach the Little Bighorn encampment from the north while Custer circled around from the southeast.

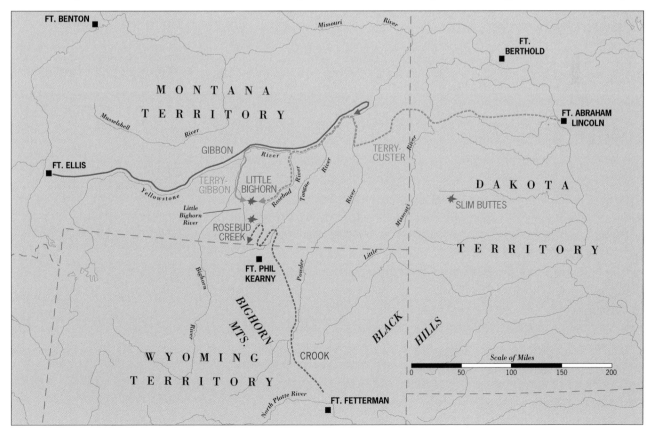

that there were bluecoats off in the distance. "We could hardly believe that the soldiers were so near," Runs the Enemy observed later. Once they had repulsed Crook's force, the Indians assumed that the soldiers were in retreat. In any case, no enemies they knew of—Indian or wasichu—would attack at the height of the day, when they could more effectively steal up in the dark and strike at dawn. Runs the Enemy and his companions returned to their pipes, and the late sleepers dozed on.

By noon Custer had made his way down into the river valley, but his view to the west was blocked by hills and swales. He paused and sent three companies under Captain Frederick Benteen off on a sweep to the southwest to hunt for hostile Indians in that direction, while the other units moved ahead. Before continuing, Custer also assigned three companies and most of the Indian scouts to his immediate subordinate, Major Reno, and kept the remaining five companies under his personal command—a move evidently motivated by Custer's belief that the Indians would run as soon as they were pressured and that a divided force would be needed to corral them.

By two o'clock in the afternoon, Custer and Reno had approached to within a few miles of the Little Bighorn and could see a big dust cloud off to the northwest. Interpreter Frank Girard rode to the top of a knoll to get a better view and spotted an Indian party galloping away toward the river. "Here are your Indians, running like devils," Girard called to Custer. The colonel asked a Crow scout about the dust cloud and received a similar answer. Only a camp on the move could kick up so much dust, the scout concluded. "The Sioux must be running away."

Custer relayed verbal orders to Reno to cross the river and attack in

In a sketch by Sioux artist Amos Bad Heart Bull, based on the recollections of warriors, Sitting Bull and Crazy Horse—his body decorated for battle with dots of hail—rally their fellow Sioux to resist the soldiers menacing the Little Bighorn camp on June 25. While Crazy Horse led men into battle against Custer's troopers, Sitting Bull stayed close to the camp to pray, reassure his warriors, and watch over their kin, as befitted a leader described by one of his followers as the "old man chief of all the camps combined."

the direction of the dust cloud from the south. Although the instructions were vague, they left Reno with no doubt that Custer would be there to back him up. In fact, the commander of the 7th Cavalry was so concerned with catching the Indians that he would soon leave Reno to his own devices and hasten northward along the east side of the river to block the presumed retreat with his five companies.

Sure of Custer's support, Reno and his 114 cavalrymen splashed across a ford in the river a short time later and galloped northward. At last they could see what they were up against. With every stride, the encampment became clearer, and the churning mass of Indians grew larger. The truth hit Reno like a thunderclap. The warriors were not running away. They were gathering in appalling numbers to meet him.

Chief Gall of the Hunkpapa Sioux, pictured in the 1880s, mounted furious assaults against the federal troops at the Little Bighorn after his two wives and three children were killed by Arikara scouts during the initial attack led by Custer's second-in-command, Major Marcus Reno. "We took no prisoners," Gall recalled. "Our hearts were bad, and we cut and shot them all to pieces."

Up ahead in the encampment, the late sleepers were waking to the peril. Wooden Leg recalled that when the first cries of distress went up, he was dozing fitfully in his lodge, dreaming of a crowd of people who were making a huge noise. "Something in the noise startled me," he said. "I found myself wide awake, sitting up and listening. My brother too awakened, and we both jumped to our feet. A great commotion was going on among the camps. We heard shooting." After hastily daubing on some war paint, Wooden Leg mounted up and headed into battle. Elsewhere in the encampment, an Oglala chief named Low Dog was roused from sleep by the cries as well. The sun was high in the sky, he recalled, and he thought some fool had panicked and raised a false alarm. "I did not think it possible that any white men would attack us, so strong as we were." When he stepped from his lodge, however, he could see that bluecoats were firing on the "end of the camp where Sitting Bull and the Hunkpapas were," and that warriors there were holding their ground "to give the women and children time to get out of the way."

Sitting Bull's Hunkpapas were indeed at

the pressure point. Located at the southern end of the encampment, their circle stood directly in Reno's path. When Sitting Bull heard the first shots, he reached for his shield—imbued with medicine to protect the chief and his people—and handed it along with his bow and war club to One Bull, his nephew and adopted son. One Bull, in return, gave Sitting Bull his pistol and his repeating rifle. As an elder and as the spiritual leader of the encampment, Sitting Bull would not conduct men into battle on this day. He would lend his moral support to the warriors, however, and use every weapon at his disposal to defend the women and children.

South of Sitting Bull's camp circle, Major Reno had prudently signaled for his men to rein in and dismount some distance from the nearest lodges. He then followed prescribed tactics and sent every fourth trooper to the rear to hold the horses and deployed the rest in a thin skirmish line, with each man about 10 feet from the next. Boldly pressing forward, the soldiers fired and reloaded as fast as they could, keeping the warriors on the defensive for a while. But then Crazy Horse arrived on the scene with a large band of Oglalas, yelling "Hoka Hey! Hoka Hey!"—"Charge! Charge!" Inspired, the mounted Indians grew bolder by the minute, swirling menacingly around the left flank of Reno's force. Seeing no sign of help from Custer, the major drew his men back into the cover of some timber near the river, but that position proved equally vulnerable. Warriors set the dry underbrush ablaze and crept in beneath the smoke. Leaping up, they fired their rifles and bows, then dropped down again. Soon Indians were encircling the force holed up in the woods; a few even made their way across the river and began firing down on the soldiers from the bluffs there.

Suddenly warriors burst into a clearing in the woods where the scout Bloody Knife was conferring with Reno and opened fire from scarcely 30 feet away. A bullet caught the scout flush in the forehead, spattering blood, brains, and bits of skull over the major. The panic rising in Reno erupted. He had just ordered his men to mount up. Now he yelled for them to dismount, only to reinstate his original order moments later. Some soldiers were too far away to see or hear their frantic commander, and more than a few were left behind when Reno and the rest of the cavalrymen bolted out of the woods and raced southeastward for the nearest river crossing— a treacherous ford with steep banks and swift water.

Warriors took up the chase, among them Wooden Leg and his fellow Cheyennes. "The soldier horses moved slowly, as if they were very tired," he recalled. "Ours were very lively. We gained rapidly on them." To the pur-

Chief Red Hawk and a group of Oglala Sioux gather on a knoll during a 1907 reenactment of the Little Bighorn battle, in which Red Hawk participated as a young man. Like the warriors involved in the 1876 battle, some of the men here bear rifles while others carry such traditional weapons as lances.

suing Indians, it was like chasing buffalo. Some rode up alongside their fleeing quarry and poured fire into the soldiers' flank. Others darted in from the rear and singled out choice targets. Wooden Leg and a Cheyenne named Little Bird set their sights on one trooper who was falling behind. Pressing in on either side, they counted coup on their hapless victim by lashing him with their pony whips. "It seemed not brave to shoot him," explained Wooden Leg. But the soldier turned his revolver and fired a shot into Little Bird's thigh. "Immediately, I whacked the white man fighter on his head with the heavy elk-horn handle of my pony whip," related Wooden Leg. "The blow dazed him. I seized the rifle strapped to his back. I wrenched it and dragged the looping strap over his head." The soldier lost his balance and lurched from the saddle. "I do not know what became of him," said Wooden Leg. "The jam of oncoming Indians swept me on."

At one point during the same furious chase, Crazy Horse—his face painted with a lightning bolt, his body dotted with hail marks—went after a soldier on a runaway horse. Swiftly he closed on the trooper and brought him down with a single blow of his heavy, stone-headed war club. Crazy Horse's 13-year-old cousin, Black Elk, was following in the wake of the attack when a warrior pointed to a wounded soldier writhing in agony on the ground. "Boy, get off and scalp him," commanded the warrior. Black Elk was inexpert and his knife was dull. The dying man groaned and ground his teeth, so Black Elk shot him in the head with his revolver and cut away the rest of his scalp.

Up ahead at the river, desperate soldiers on their mounts were plunging from the high bank into the river like buffalo being driven to destruction. A number of cavalrymen floundered in the churning water and fell victim to the furious pursuers. Indians surrounded their prey in the water and yanked them from their horses, shooting, lancing, and swinging their stone bludgeons. Some perished in the melee. Others pursued bluecoats all the way to the far bank, where Major Reno and the other survivors sought shelter atop a rugged bluff.

With more than 30 cavalrymen dead and nearly as many wounded or missing, Reno had already lost roughly half of his command. To make matters worse, all but a few of his Indian scouts had ridden off to claim ponies from the enemy herds earlier in the battle and were now out of touch. To his credit, Reno managed to restore a semblance of fighting order on top of the bluff. But he might well have been overrun had not his opponents been diverted by a fresh challenge. Up at the far end of the village, lookouts had spotted another herd of bluecoats.

Warriors are depicted driving Major Reno's retreating troopers across the Little Bighorn in a vivid painting by Amos Bad Heart Bull. A number of Reno's men, already wounded, drowned in the stream or were caught and slaughtered there by pursuing Indians. "They began to drive the soldiers all mixed up—Sioux, then soldiers, then more Sioux, and all shooting," recalled Cheyenne chief Two Moons. "I saw the soldiers fall back and drop into the riverbed like buffalo fleeing."

Since parting from Reno, Custer had led his five companies northward until he reached high ground that afforded him a view of the big encampment across the river. From there, he had seen Reno's men approaching from the south and the resulting turmoil in the dust-shrouded village. What Custer did next remains something of a mystery, for he and his men were destined for an obliterating encounter that would leave gaps in the historical record. Evidently he still believed the Indians would wilt, and he was determined to cut off their expected retreat. He did not wait to see how Reno's attack developed. Instead he dispatched a messenger to summon Benteen, along with the trailing packtrain; then he pressed on toward the northern end of the encampment.

While Custer pushed ahead, Reno was being driven back toward the river. Few warriors who took part in that chase would soon forget the moment when they realized that a second and potentially greater challenge awaited them to the north. The Lakota Runs the Enemy—who earlier had ignored reports that soldiers were nearby—was returning to the camp after pursuing Reno's men when he saw two Indians on the east side of the river waving blankets in warning. Runs the Enemy rode over to speak with them. They yelled out to him that the "genuine stuff was coming," as he put it later, and that the women and children were again in danger. The source of their dismay was soon evident. Looking to the northeast, Runs the Enemy saw that the ridge was aswarm with bluecoats. Sadly, he concluded that Reno's attack had been a diversion and that the big blow was about to fall. Gathering his men around him, Runs the Enemy sensed their fear. He decided to strip himself of his finery and fight alongside them like a plain warrior: "I took off the ribbons from my hair, also my shirt and pants, and threw them away, saving nothing but my belt of cartridges and gun. I thought, most of the Sioux will fall today; I will fall with them."

Just then, Sitting Bull rode by on his buckskin horse and calmly reminded the nervous warriors of their duty. He urged them to be like the bird who spies the enemy and "spreads its wing to cover the nest and eggs and protect them. We are here to protect our wives and children, and we must not let the soldiers get them." Then Sitting Bull rode from band to band, calling out, "Make a brave fight!" Heeding his words and the cries of their war leaders, more than 1,000 warriors forded the Little Bighorn and made their way up the hillside.

It soon became apparent that the soldiers menacing the encampment were vastly outnumbered. To make matters worse for Custer, his forces were strung out along the ridge. The commander had moved ahead with two of his companies, evidently intent on locating a river crossing north of the encampment. The other three companies occupied positions to the south of Custer's, and those trailing units were the first to be overwhelmed. For some time, they had been harassed by small bands of warriors, but now a multitude of fighting men swept up the ridge toward them like a storm surge. A few warriors dashed about on their ponies, showing courage. But most of them advanced on foot, working their way through the tall grass and brush. Soldiers greeted them with crashing volleys, but the warriors crept closer, firing arcing shots with their bows and quick bursts from their repeating carbines.

In a bold effort to turn the tide, the company farthest south galloped partway down the hill and formed a skirmish line, with some men holding the horses while the rest advanced and fired. It was the same tactic Reno had employed earlier—and it met with a similar response. After recovering from the initial shock, warriors stood fast and gathered courage. "Come!" a Cheyenne chief named Lame White Man cried out. "We can kill all of them!" With a rush, hundreds of Indians closed on the exposed cavalrymen. In the tumult, the troopers' mounts were stampeded, and the surviving soldiers fled in confusion back up the ridge.

Once again, Crazy Horse picked the perfect moment to enter the fray. On their way back through the encampment to meet this new threat, Crazy Horse and his followers had raised the ancient Lakota battle cry: "Hoka Hey! Hoka Hey! There is never a better time to die." Now they put their lives on the line. Riding up the hillside, Crazy Horse and White Bull, a Miniconjou nephew of Sitting Bull, made a daring charge on horseback around the northern flank of the trailing units and emerged unscathed to their rear, inspiring other warriors to follow. Confronted with envelopment, the blue lines crumbled. Soldiers ran "like scared rabbits," White Bull recollected. A few escaped north to join Custer's men, but most fell prey to the swarming attackers. Here and there, stranded troopers stood their ground, revolvers in hand. Guns flashed in the midst of the thickening pall of dust and smoke, their roar mixing with the death cries of soldiers and the warriors' whoops and piercing eagle-bone war whistles.

About a half-mile to the north, Custer had halted his vanguard below a crest known thenceforth as Custer's Hill. From there he could hear the din of fire that signaled trouble for the trailing units. But if he realized how desperate their situation was, there was little he could do about it. Hundreds of warriors were pressing uphill through the tall grass toward his two meager companies. Custer ordered one company to dismount and form a skirmish line while holding the other unit in reserve. But his opponents shrewdly set out to separate the dismounted cavalrymen from their horses. While some warriors harried the skirmishers on foot, others galloped forward on painted war ponies, yelling and waving blankets to panic the soldiers' mounts. Among the attacking Sioux were 30 or so zealous young men who had vowed to "throw their lives away." Dashing up the ridge, they rushed into the line of fire and smashed through the skirmishers, completing the stampede of their horses.

Custer and his men hastily retreated up the hill. There frantic survivors of the three rearguard companies reached them, sowing terror among the

Relics of unknown warriors who opposed the bluecoats at the Little Bighorn include the war club shown at top, its rawhide-wrapped handle decorated with bands of colored beads; and the handsome Sioux war bonnet above, with two ermine pendants, a beaded brim, and 32 eagle feathers in its crown, each representing a deed of valor.

The stage was set for a catastrophe at the Little Bighorn when Custer divided his force. He first dispatched Captain Frederick Benteen on a scouting mission, then sent Reno and his men to attack the southern end of the Indian encampment while leading his own battalion north along the ridge to cut off an anticipated retreat. Instead, the warriors rallied and turned on their attackers in overwhelming numbers, first driving Reno's surviving troopers up a bluff on the east bank of the river and then annihilating Custer's units.

backpedaling soldiers. Custer, who had been so intent on enveloping the opposition, saw now that the tables had been turned. His was a plight an officer wiser in the ways of Indian fighting men might have anticipated: The front was all around, and the rear was nowhere.

As warriors closed in for the kill, some soldiers took cover behind dead horses and postponed the inevitable. But soon Indians came groping through the pall of battle to finish them off with knives and clubs. In desperation, a group of about 30 surviving troopers scrambled down the slope on foot and sought shelter in a coulee. A mass of warriors made up largely of Hunkpapas converged on this Deep Ravine—as it was known thereafter—and turned it into a deathtrap. With cries of triumph, Sitting Bull's followers fired down into the bluecoats and annihilated them.

The carnage along the ridge surpassed anything in the warriors' experience. "Smoke rolled up like a mountain above our heads," recalled Runs the Enemy. "The soldiers were piled one on top of another, dead, with here and there an Indian among the soldiers. Horses lay on top of men and men

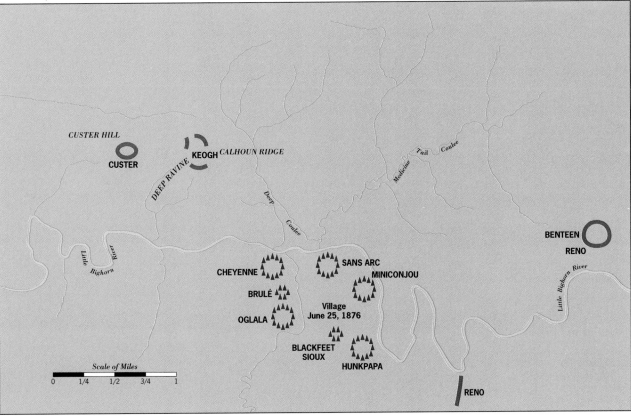

on top of horses." When the smoke cleared, George Armstrong Custer and all 210 men of the five companies he led into the fray were dead or dying.

Afterward, distraught women and youngsters from the encampment—many of whom had lost loved ones to the bluecoats—mutilated the soldiers' bodies with knives, lances, and clubs, adding to the grim work already performed by warriors claiming scalps and other trophies. Other Indians stripped the dead of useful clothing and keepsakes and claimed their weapons and ammunition. Yet there was little jubilation in the camp circles that evening. Sitting Bull's followers had won a great victory, yet they had much to mourn—at least 30 warriors had been killed and dozens more wounded. Nor had all the bluecoats been dispatched. Reno and his men remained on the bluff, where they had been driven earlier in the day and where they had since been reinforced by Benteen's three companies, which Custer had hoped for in vain.

Benteen had linked up with Reno shortly after the major's frantic retreat across the river. Stunned by the strength of their opposition, the two officers had elected to remain where they were until the ammunition-laden packtrain arrived. By the time they moved out in an effort to join forces with Custer, the battle to the north was all but over. From atop the ridge, they could see in the distance a churning mass of Indians, "riding around and firing at objects on the ground," as one officer later testified.

Slashing with a saber, his long hair waving, Custer fights bravely to the end in one of many romanticized depictions of the "last stand" that were executed by white artists after the battle. In fact, Custer did not carry a saber—he was armed with a rifle, a pair of pistols, and a hunting knife—and he had cropped his hair before the campaign.

They knew something was amiss, but they could not imagine that in fact they were witnessing the end of Custer's command.

Seeing warriors approaching to renew hostilities, Reno and Benteen retreated to their original position on the bluff. Hastily the cavalrymen dug in behind packs and hardtack boxes. A firefight raged until dusk and started up again at dawn on June 26, but the Sioux and Cheyennes found the entrenched troopers hard to get at. "The soldiers had burrowed into the ground like prairie dogs," complained one Sioux chief. By noon the attackers were eager to move on and left the bluecoats to count their grievous losses. In less than 24 hours, the defiant Indians had cut the 7th U.S. Cavalry Regiment in half, killing 263 men and wounding another 59.

Through the day, women in the encampment packed up their belongings and bundled them onto travois poles lashed to ponies, leaving behind only the possessions of the dead, which they abandoned according to custom. Then the allied bands headed southward in a great stream, away

Custer loses his saber—and his heroic stature—in this drawing by an Indian artist showing Long Hair, as the Sioux had called him, being felled by a mounted warrior's lance. Actually, Custer, who died of bullet wounds to the chest and temple, was not identified by his enemies until after the battle. "The excitement was so great that we scarcely recognized our nearest friends," a warrior named Rain in the Face remarked. "Everything was done like lightning."

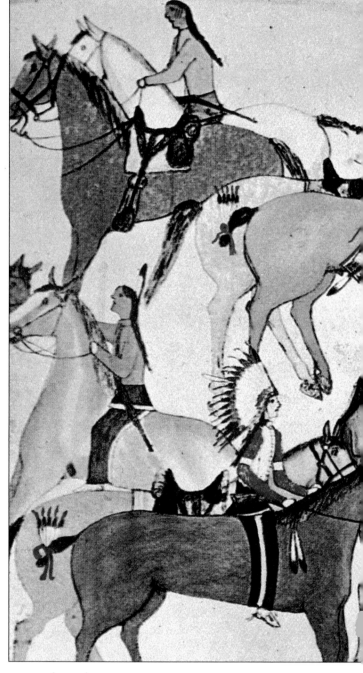

from a big soldier force that their scouts warned them was approaching. "Again, as at all other times, the Cheyennes went ahead," Wooden Leg recalled. Bringing up the rear were the Hunkpapas of Sitting Bull—the holy man who had shielded them with his prayers.

A week or so after the Battle of the Little Bighorn, the leaders of the various hunting bands met with Sitting Bull in council and resolved to separate. They had little choice, for such a vast encampment could not long sustain itself. Small parties could better follow the elusive buffalo herds without exhausting forage and fuel.

By dispersing, the chiefs may have also hoped to frustrate their pursuers. General Terry, who reached the battle site with Colonel Gibbon from the north on June 27, was appalled by what he found and took time to regroup. When Terry and Crook finally resumed operations in early August, they were back where they started—pursuing hunting bands across a wide area. Some Indians who had left the agencies in June chose to return there. But many of the others held out, including Sitting Bull's Hunkpapas and Crazy Horse's Oglalas.

Terry and Crook—with nearly 3,500 troops and 325 Indian auxiliaries between them—followed separate paths but met with similar frustrations. Terry concluded his campaign on September 5 without having fought a single battle. The closest Crook came to victory was on September 9, when a detachment of 150 cavalrymen captured a small Lakota camp at Slim Buttes in the Dakota Territory. As it happened, Crazy Horse was encamped nearby and struck back the next day with several hundred of his warriors, who swarmed about so furiously that Crook had to deploy his force of nearly 2,000 men in a square to hold them off. On September 11, Crook left the captured village in flames and set off with his tired and hungry men for the Black Hills, where Crook, too, ended his pursuit.

Yet the campaign to crush Indian resistance on the Northern Plains would only intensify, for the carnage at the Little Bighorn had infuriated federal authorities. General Sherman in July had persuaded Congress to place the reservations under the absolute control of the army. Indian

Taking the spoils of victory at the Little Bighorn, Indian warriors lead away saddled army horses in another painting by Amos Bad Heart Bull. "After the battle, we young men were chasing horses all over the prairie," recalled Rain in the Face, "while the old men and women plundered the bodies."

agents in the troubled region were replaced with army officers, who treated all Indians on the reservations as potentially hostile. Weapons, ammunition, and ponies were confiscated, and some men were held as prisoners of war, while others were induced to serve as scouts in future forays against the defiant bands. Then on August 15, President Grant signed into law a bill forbidding the payment of a single penny of the year's appropriations—one million dollars for food alone—to any branch of the Sioux engaged in hostilities, a provision that applied even to Indians who had kept peace while others of their faction resisted. Moreover, future appropriations would be withheld until the Sioux ced-

A STINT ON STAGE

In one of history's strange twists, Sitting Bull, the Lakota chief who led the resistance to U.S. forces in 1876, later performed with the gaudiest extravaganza ever to come out of the Plains, William F. "Buffalo Bill" Cody's hugely popular Wild West Show. Wearing his full chief's regalia while Cody donned his version of Western duds, as seen at left, Sitting Bull was introduced with great fanfare at performances and received thunderous applause from audiences despite his long history of defying white men and their way of life.

Sitting Bull's reasons for taking part in Cody's show were various. Following the Battle of the Little Bighorn, he had spent four years as a refugee in Canada, then two years as a prisoner of war at Fort Randall, then two more at the Standing Rock Agency. He joined Cody in 1885 for a measure of freedom, for money that he shared with the needy, for the acclaim he won from audiences—and for the insights he gained into the world of the white man. Furthermore, he admired Buffalo Bill, a former hunter and scout who treated all the Indians in the show with respect and paid special deference to Sitting Bull as a great chief.

None of this altered Sitting Bull's nature. After touring for a while, he returned to the Standing Rock Agency and declined a later invitation from Cody to rejoin the show. "I am needed here," Sitting Bull explained. "There is more talk of taking our lands."

ed much of their existing territory and agreed to railroad rights of way across the remaining land, among other conditions.

The message was clear: Surrender or starve. On September 20, a delegation of discouraged chiefs—29 Sioux and five Cheyennes, most of them agency leaders—were driven to "touch the pen," as they called it, and endorse the terms imposed on them.

The signees did not include Sitting Bull, Crazy Horse, or other champions of resistance. The final blows against them came from the army in the form of a brutally effective winter campaign, aided by Indians recently recruited on the reservations. In late November, Colonel Ranald Mackenzie, a veteran of the Red River War, mustered a force of 1,100 men, including nearly 400 Indians, and surprised a large camp of some 1,500 Cheyennes near the Bighorn Mountains. Those villagers had recently sent warriors to raid a Shoshone village, and they were not surprised to see members of that enemy tribe fighting for the bluecoats. But the presence of Cheyenne recruits among the attacking force shocked and demoralized them. Driven from their camp, many of them perished in the cold before the survivors found shelter with Crazy Horse's Oglalas on the Tongue River.

Meanwhile, another seasoned Indian fighter, Colonel Nelson Miles, had joined in the pursuit of the defiant hunting bands. In December his forces destroyed Sitting Bull's camp at Redwater Creek in eastern Montana and sent the Hunkpapas fleeing to join Crazy Horse as well. Then in January, Miles and his men—wearing coats made of buffalo robes taken from Sitting Bull's camp—clashed with the holdouts in the midst of a brewing snowstorm. Their camp was dispersed, and the fugitives knew now that the federal pursuit would continue relentlessly—and that they could expect no support from the reservations, where the soldier chiefs were in full control. In May of 1877, Crazy Horse acknowledged defeat and led his Oglalas and their Cheyenne allies to the Red Cloud Agency in Wyoming, where they surrendered. Later that year, the army responded to rumors that Crazy Horse was plotting trouble again by sending soldiers to lock him up. The great war chief resisted, and a soldier bayoneted him to death.

Sitting Bull, for his part, soon sought refuge with his remaining followers across the border in Canada, where they pursued buffalo on the open plains for a time. But authorities there ultimately forced them back to the only harbor left for them—the reservation they had fought so hard to avoid. For Sitting Bull, years of bitter concessions lay ahead, until he too, like Crazy Horse, was accused of rekindling the spirit of defiance among his people and was shot dead while resisting arrest. ◆

Although adapted to the ways of whites, who knew him as Jack Wilson, Wovoka of the Paiute had a revelation that made him a messiah to oppressed Indians.

LEGACY OF THE GHOST DANCE

"The sun died," said Wovoka of the day he had his vision. The Paiute holy man related that he fell into a trance when the sky darkened (probably during the solar eclipse of January 1, 1889) and was taken to heaven, where all the Indians who had died were alive again. God told him, he said, that Indians on earth who never lied or stole, and who lived in peace, would join their ancestors in this native paradise. And they could hasten the reunion by means of a special dance.

Wovoka recounted his vision and taught his people the new Ghost Dance and songs to accompany it. His blend of Christian and Indian traditions—along with his promise of a world free of pain, disease, and white men—held potent appeal for an afflicted people. But the intensity with which they embraced the doctrine was jarring to nervous whites, who assumed that such fervor would turn hostile. Despite its peaceful origins, the Ghost Dance brought terrible punishment to the Sioux at Wounded Knee.

Arapahos perform the Ghost Dance in a rare picture taken by James Mooney, a U.S. government anthropologist who was among the few people ever permitted to photograph the ceremony.

Ghost Dancers proclaimed their faith by means of the finery they wore. The Arapaho buckskin dress shown above was bedecked with star symbols and eagle feathers to honor soaring spirits.

VISIONS OF REBIRTH

"They cleared off a place in the form of a circus ring," recounted a Cheyenne called Porcupine when speaking of an early Ghost Dance, so named for its promise of reunion with the dead. The dancers joined hands in a circle and for four consecutive nights shuffled from right to left, praying and chanting: "Father, I come; Mother, I come." In a break with tradition, no drums or instruments were used, and women were permitted to dance among the men.

According to the account of an Indian agent, "When the dancers were worn out, the medicine men would shout that they could see the faces of departed friends and relatives moving about the circle. No pen can paint the picture of wild excitement that ensued."

A Cheyenne hide painting depicts the key elements of the Ghost Dance: the dancers shuffling hand in hand, with exhausted or entranced dancers inside the circle.

After being ceremonially painted (top), Arapaho Ghost Dancers sing of dead friends and of the days when buffalo were plentiful, in scenes that were photographed by James Mooney in 1893. Many of the dancers entered trances in which they reported seeing their ancestors.

DIVINE PROTECTION

"In 1889 the Oglala heard that the son of God had come upon earth in the west," recounted Lakota George Sword of South Dakota's Pine Ridge Reservation. The Sioux sent delegates across the Rocky Mountains to investigate. In the spring of 1890, they returned home with a version of the Ghost Dance different from that taught by Wovoka.

As the Sioux took up the ritual, they added to it a preliminary purification of each dancer in a sweat lodge and a ceremonial pole, or tree, for the center of

Fearing retribution from authorities, Sioux Ghost Dancers carried objects that had long offered protection to warriors, such as this buckskin shield bearing the image of an owl and the feathers of an eagle. The Sioux also wore the Ghost Shirt, which was supposed to shield the wearer from harm, as portrayed in a ledger drawing of a rider galloping unscathed through a hail of bullets (right).

the dance circle. In a more significant change, the Sioux espoused a militant faith. Accordingly, dance leaders preached that in order to fulfill the promise of an Indian paradise in the next world, God would wipe white men from the face of the earth. Although the Sioux peoples did not intend to be the agents of the white man's destruction, they did fear violence from authorities. To protect themselves from harm, the Ghost Dancers wore a decorated garment they called the Ghost Shirt, thought to be impenetrable.

The Oglala Sioux delegates Kicking Bear (top) and Short Bull led a party of five other Sioux from the Dakota Territory to far-off Nevada to look into accounts of an Indian messiah. They reported that Wovoka had been crucified by whites and had returned to life to redeem Indians.

AWAITING WORLD'S END

In late 1890, some 20,000 hungry Sioux on four Dakota reservations were languishing on "alkali land and government rations," as one official put it. Fervently, they took up the Ghost Dance and awaited the day of reckoning, expected in the spring of 1891. Fearing that the dancers might resort to violence to fulfill the prophecy of doom for whites, authorities tried to end the movement by calling in federal troops. Some Indians sought refuge in the Badlands. Others, including followers of Sitting Bull, stayed put and trusted in their protective Ghost Shirts.

Moved by a private vision, an enraptured Sioux Ghost Dancer leaves the big dance circle in this painting by Frederic Remington, who based the scene on recollections of a Ghost Dance he had witnessed.

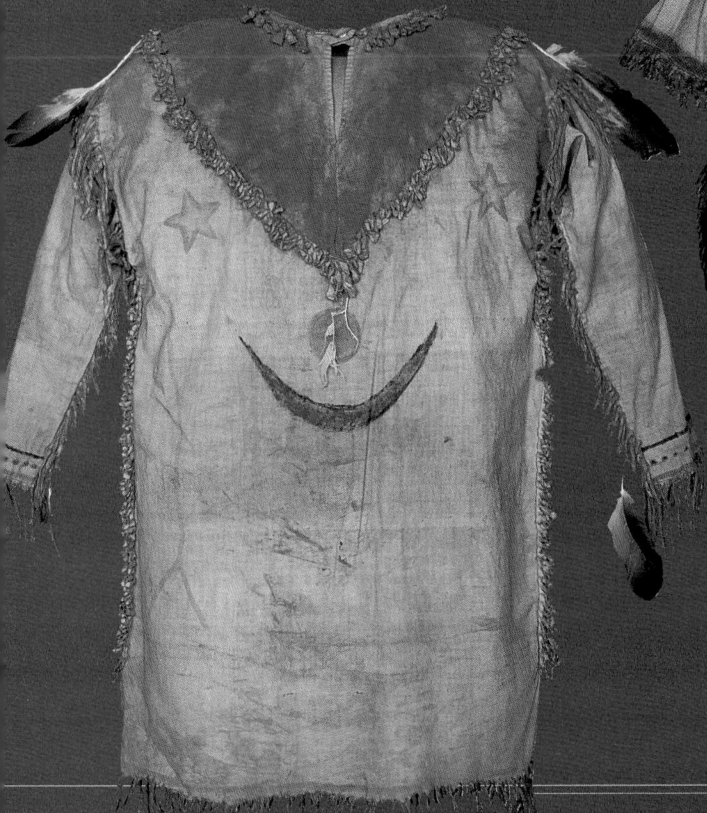

Makers of Sioux Ghost Shirts employed traditional methods, cutting the white man's muslin (used in the shirts shown here) as if it were a hide, and sewing it with animal sinew. Decorations were individual and varied, but they relied heavily on two symbols with special meaning for the Sioux—stars and eagle feathers.

SITTING BULL IS DEAD.

The Old Chief and Seven of His Followers Killed in an Engagement with Police.

Sitting Bull was Preparing to Start for the Bad Lands and His Arrest was Ordered.

The Indian Police Start From Yates, Followed by Two Companies—Cavalry and Infantry.

When the Arrest was Made, Sitting Bull's Followers Attempted a Recapture.

In the Fight That Ensued, Sitting Bull, His Son and Six Indians were Killed.

On the Other Side, Four of the Police were Killed and Three Wounded.

The Cavalry Then Arrived on the Scene, and the Indians Fled Up Grand River.

A Lengthy Account of Major McLaughlin's Last Trip to Sitting Bull's Camp.

He's a Good Indian Now.

CHICAGO, Dec. 15.—At 9 o'clock to-night, Assistant Adjutant General Corbin of General Miles' staff received an official dispatch from St. Paul, saying Sitting Bull, five of Sitting Bull's men and seven of the Indian police have been killed. Thirteen casualties were the result of the attempt by the Indian police to arrest Sitting Bull.

HOW IT HAPPENED.

ST. PAUL, Dec. 15—The report was received in this city this afternoon that Sitting Bull had been killed by Indian po-

Newspapers across the country trumpeted the death of Sitting Bull and lionized the Indian policeman Red Tomahawk (at right, center) who shot him.

DEATH OF A CHIEFTAIN

When word of the Ghost Dance first reached him at the Standing Rock Agency, Sitting Bull was skeptical. "It is impossible," he declared, "for a dead man to return and live again." He soon recognized, however, that ghost dancing was restoring the spirits of demoralized Sioux, and he embraced the movement. Alarmed, Indian agent James McLaughlin first tried to persuade Sitting Bull to reject the ritual. When that failed, he set out to separate the movement's "high priest," as he called Sitting Bull, from his followers.

On December 14, 1890, the agent dispatched Sioux policemen to arrest Sitting Bull. The next morning, they surrounded the old chief's cabin and seized him. He balked at their rough handling, and shooting broke out between his followers and the police. When it was over, Sitting Bull lay dead, along with seven of his band—including his son Crow Foot—and six Indian policemen.

A Sioux depiction of the death of Sitting Bull, painted on muslin, shows the chief being dragged from his cabin (center) by three blue-coated policemen. When two of them fell mortally wounded, the third executed Sitting Bull. Outnumbered three to one, the police held off enraged Sioux for two hours, until troops arrived.

Chief Big Foot (right) and his band—photographed above in August 1890, five months before they were surrounded at Wounded Knee—tried to avoid confrontation with soldiers until the Ghost Dance prophecies came to pass.

MASSACRE AT WOUNDED KNEE

Dismayed by Sitting Bull's death and the approach of troops, the Sioux chief Big Foot and his band of 350 people—many of them Ghost Dancers—fled their homes near the Cheyenne River Agency and made for the Badlands. The 7th Cavalry gave chase. When troops caught up with them on December 28, the Sioux surrendered. The next morning, 470 soldiers who had surrounded their camp along Wounded Knee Creek ordered them to give up their guns. As tense troops scoured tipis, a medicine man urged people to be strong. One Sioux grappled with soldiers trying to disarm him, and his gun went off. Shooting erupted on both sides, and many Indians fled in terror. "We tried to run," said one woman, "but they shot us like we were buffalo." The massacre claimed the lives of nearly 200 Sioux, most of them women and children.